THE BRACEROS

Guest Workers, Settlers, and Family Legacies

Paul López

Kendall Hunt
publishing company

Cover photos provided by the author.

www.kendallhunt.com
Send all inquiries to:
4050 Westmark Drive
Dubuque, IA 52004-1840

Printed in the United States of America
10 9 8 7 6 5 4 3 2

Contents

Acknowledgments

From the start this book has been a collective effort. However, any errors in the conclusions reached should be solely attributed to me. I would first like to thank the former Mexican braceros who shared their time and their tremendous oral histories. Their stories gave me new insight into the history of the program. The stories were remarkable given the amount of time that had passed since the demise of the program. I can't thank them enough for allowing me to spend time with them as they recalled their personal experiences. Lasting more than two hours, they were more than willing to recount their participation in the program. Welcoming me into their homes, where the interviews tended to occur, was more than I could ever ask in terms of their generosity. For their time and, of course, their great stories, I am forever grateful. My one wish is to do justice to their stories as former immigrant guest workers.

One of the enjoyments of academic life is having the opportunity to collect and write up the results of one's research. During the spring of 2001, I was offered a post-doctoral fellowship at the Center for Chicano Studies at the University of California, Santa Barbara. Besides allowing me to return to the city where I was born and raised, the fellowship provided the ideal setting for conducting the research and writing the initial chapters of the book manuscript. The fellowship released me from my teaching responsibilities so often a major responsibility for CSU faculty. Teaching a full load of classes each semester take its toll on being able to produce scholarly work. I would like to thank the following faculty members at the Center of Chicano Studies and the Department of Chicano Studies at UCSB for their kind assistance and support while in residence. First, I would like to thank the Director of the Center for Chicano Studies, Professor Carl Guterriez-Jones. The moment the fellowship was offered, Carl was always so gracious with his time. Thank you so much Carl!

I would next like to offer a "special" thanks to Professor Mario T. Garcia. Mario was extremely gracious with his time and his efforts to support the project. Indeed, Mario's insight into the process of oral history as a research method was tremendously helpful. Having a senior scholar in the field of Chicano Studies who offered suggestions and valued criticism was a tremendous boast to the book's completion. *Muchas gracias* Mario!

I would also like to thank Marta Barjaras for helping along the way. She helped to coordinate recruiting efforts by advertising my project to other potential contacts. Thank you, Marta.

The staff at the Center was also extremely helpful. Thank you, Anne Ewell for managing the tapes as they were being transcribed. I could always count on Anne for keeping the students busy with the next set of tapes to be transcribed. I would also like to thank Karen Cisernos for the help she provided during my stay at the Center. You two were so wonderful while I was in residence.

While at the Center I was able to hire three students to do the transcribing of the bracero interviews. Many thanks, to Alberto Feliciano, Carla Galinedez, and Carmen Cuevas. One of my interviewees was Carmen's grandfather. I was also able to have the following students at Chico State do some additional transcribing: Thank you Jessica Ocegueda, Lizzette Garcia, Stephanie Godoy, Alex Gradilla, Miguel Guerrero, Miguel Ceballos, Roque Guerrero, and Felix Medina. Thanks to Vito Tenorio who designed the website on my bracero project. Thank you so much Vito!

I also wish to extend a warm thanks to the following colleagues and friends who have offered encouragement toward the completion of the project: Professors and colleagues, Alberto López Pulido, Robert De Anda, Barbara Driscoll de Alvarado, Manuel Barjaras, Jesus "El Jefe" Rosales, and Geraldo Mireles.

To my *familia* in the northern periphery of California, I want to first thank Dr. Vincent Ornelas. Vince has been a friend, mentor, colleague, and overall just a great guy to be with. Although we are both university professors, it has been remarkable how we have been able to bond as friends. If we had met as childhood friends, I know it would have been a long lasting friendship. We share so many similarities growing up. Even though we both root for different college teams, I always enjoy his insights on life and work. I know he has made, and continues to make, remarkable progress as a university professor. To my extended *familia* in Chico: Ignacio "Buddy" Vargas, Anna Vargas, Irene Ornelas, Manuel Palmarin, and Allen Luedecke. We have shared many good times, and I appreciate their encouragement and support of the book.

Special recognition goes to Dr. Susan Marie Green. While on academic leave (2001-2002), it was up to my colleague to "man" the Chicano Studies program at Chico State. Activist, mom, colleague, friend, mentor, CFA union chapter president, Chicano Studies scholar—she wears many hats. I would also like to thank her kids, Clare Green and Alex Green for all the fun times together. Since her arrival to Chico State in 1999, she has made a big difference on the Chico State campus and beyond. Anyone who has met her and has talked with her for more than a few minutes does not soon forget her. She is a remarkable person. I can't express how much she has meant to the completion of the book. She read and commented on the manuscript. While on leave, she more than adequately upheld the program's growth and course offerings. Besides teaching her normal set of courses in Chicano Studies, Susan also took on the courses I regularly teach. Not surprisingly, she did a marvelous job. Indeed, while on academic leave, Susan earned two faculty awards for her professional achievement and faculty advisement with MEChA (*Movimiento Estudiantil Chicano de Aztlán*) students. I want to thank you so much for being there when the project was in its embryo stage and worked its way through the completion.

I also want to thank the MEChA students with whom I work very closely at Chico State. Since serving as faculty advisor over the years to the student group MEChA (*Movimiento Estudiantil Chicanos Aztlán*), I have enjoyed the warmth of their energy as they completed their college education. I want to thank Cesar Lara, Esperanza "Espy" Sandoval, Rosanna Polanco, Fabian Alvarez, Gabe Lechuqa, Angie Cisneros, Gonzalo Ortega, Elia Moreno, Sabrina Rascon, Yesica Ramirez, Lizette Perez, Adrian Garcia, Tanya Roberts, Karina

Conteras, Alex Gradilla, Jesus Torres, Monica Leonard, Jaime Barjaras, Blas Tenorio Jr., Miguel Melendez, Savahana Lamp, Victor López, Sonia Robles, and Jesus Cortez.

I would like to extend a special thanks to the Director of the Oral History Institute at the University of Texas-El Paso, Kristine Navarro. Kristine has been so generous with allowing me to store my oral hsitories and also helping me to collect additional oral histories. I want extend a big *abrazo* to her for her help with this research project.

There are few organizations that provide a space for presenting work in Chicano Studies. I have found the National Association for Chicana and Chicano Studies organization one of the few that provides a space and peers who share my similar scholarly interests. I would like to thank NACCS for providing opportunities to present my bracero research. A special thanks to Kathy Blackmeyer-Reyes, Dr. Rhonda Rios-Kravitz, and Dr. Julia Curry-Rodriguez for making NACCS an annual special event to meet with colleagues and friends who share my research interest in Chicano Studies.

I would also like to thank the students who were part of Chicano Studies courses at Chico State over the last couple of years, who encouraged me to complete the project. They would often allow me to talk about the project and their continued interest was important to me. The talks with my students would often lead to increased contacts, as they would mention relatives who had been part of the program. Colleagues also at Chico State would inform me of their family's participation in the program; some of the more recent interviews have been the fathers or grandfathers of my colleagues at Chico State. I want to thank the following colleagues for their input and access to potential interviews: *Mucho gracias* to Jose Balderama, Miguel Sahagun, Dr. Norma Rodriguez, and Maggie Sahagun.

I want to thank my colleagues in the Sociology Department and the Multi-Cultural and Gender Studies Program at Chico State. The secretaries over the years who managed and maintained my various expense accounts to travel to professional meetings and interview trips (especially Maureen Knowlton) in order to complete this project.

I want to thank the publishers at Kendall/Hunt for their patience with me as I finished the final manuscript. I want to thank Katie Riggs and Dr. Frank Fornier. You guys did a great job on the cover and the rest of the manuscript.

I want to thank the folks at PBS for allowing me to be a part of the documentary, *Los Braceros: Strong Arms to Aid to the USA,* the video of the former Bracero Program.

I want to thank my *familia* in Santa Barbara, beginning with my parents, Carmen and Benny López. Both my parents opened their home to me once again while I was in residence at the Center for Chicano Studies. It had been quite some time since I last stayed more than a few days while visiting my parents. My parents provided not only for me to stay during the academic year, but also my two daughters Saundra and AnnaAlicia. For them it was a time to be even closer to their granddaughters. I know both my daughters will not forget the time that they spent with their grandparents. I love you both. I want to acknowledge my older siblings. My brother, Oswald D. López, who is successful in his own right and has been very supportive of the project and whose photo on the bracero truck appears on the back of the book. My sister, Cynthia Marie Castaneda, and her husband Richard and their three children, Christina,

Stephen, and Selena. On my trips back to Santa Barbara from Chico I could count on a *great time* to get away from the project to be among my family.

I would also like to thank my oldest child, James, for allowing me to spend so much time away from him while I was in Santa Barbara, while he stayed back in Chico during my fellowship. I hope that he knows that he is always in my thoughts, even though the project and the year apart gave me little time to see him. I love you son.

Finally, I want to thank the programs over the years that have meant so much to me. I am a former student of Affirmative Action. It was the efforts of Affirmative Action programs that enabled me to attend and complete college. I am at heart a working class individual. Although I am a university professor today, I still yearn for my working class roots. I hope in some small way my book helps those who came as working class immigrants and set the stage for their social mobility into the American mainstream. *Si Se Puede!*

Paul López
Chico, CA. 2009

I want to dedicate this book to my parents, Benny and Carmen López. Throughout their lives they've shown love and support for their kids and (great) grandkids. We are all grateful for them always being there for us.

Con mucho amor, tu hijo, Paul

Introduction

This book began from a family discussion involving my parents one summer a few years back. We were discussing their lives during the decades of the 1940s through the early 1960s. Each decade marked important events which impacted the lives of Mexican Americans. Some of the major events from that period were the United States involvement in World War II, the Zoot-Suit Riots, the U.S.-Mexico Bracero Program (1942-1964), "Operation Wetback," and the origins of the forthcoming Chicano Movement of the 1960s (Sanchez, 1996; Takaki, 2001; Garcia 1981, 1989; Acuna, 2007; Munoz, 1989). Although it has been many years since those events occurred, the eras remain open to investigation. My parents were among the many Mexican Americans whose lives were transformed by the period which was coined by Chicano historian Mario T. Garcia (1989) as the "Mexican American Generation."

My parents were both born in the United States, but experienced life from a "Mexican" working class perspective[1]. Their personal life stories revealed much about the time they lived together as husband and wife. But, it also revealed how they were a part of social history. For example, my mom worked in the packinghouses in the city of Goleta, California. According to her collective memory, she began working at the age of fifteen. She worked there until she turned eighteen and married my father. She, like so many other young Mexican American women, took what jobs were available and the packinghouses were more than willing to hire young Mexican American women. The local packing houses were owned by the Johnson Fruit Company. The packinghouses were centrally located near the local railroad lines, allowing them to ship their produce to other parts of the country.[2]

My father was born in Lamont, Colorado. Although a U.S. citizen, he returned to Mexico with his family when he was about six or seven years old. My grandparents migrated early to the United States due to the chaos of the Mexican Revolution. Spending his primary years in Mexico and following his completion of high school, my father eventually joined the Mexican military. He returned more *Mexican* than when he left as a Mexican American. He was about twenty-seven years old when he moved to Santa Barbara, California to be near his mother.[3] Upon returning to the United States, my father took on several jobs. One of his first jobs was

---

[1] Whether born in the United States or Mexico, most Americans continued to view Mexican Americans as outsiders and so the term *Mexican* was more common to describe them.

[2] Local packinghouses were relevant to other young Mexican American women as it put them in contact with braceros. Indeed, the interviews with braceros for this book revealed their chance to meet with local women from the packinghouses who later became their wives.

[3] My grandparents had divorced and my grandmother returned to the United States sometime after their return to Mexico in the 1930s. The reparations of Mexican Americans and Mexicans in the 1930s led to their movement back to the United States.

working for the city of Santa Barbara. My father described how he worked on the building of the local freeway overpass in Santa Barbara:

> . . . *I think I worked about two to three years at the overpass because there were a lot of guys there that I know because of my cousin. He said do you want to work as a laborer because I didn't know any kind of work, you know especially labor. He said, "Hey, come on, let me show you how to do it." So I went over there and from there after they finished we started looking for a job and everything and then we didn't have hardly nothing to do, we went to pick lemons a little bit and then that was already in the '50s.*
>
> (Interviewed with Benny López 2003)

Shortly after picking in the fields, my father was hired as a ranch hand in Goleta. With my mom and their three children, he worked on the ranch from 1951 to 1961. During that period, he served as an interpreter to the immigrant guest workers who were brought by truck each morning to work. Not surprisingly, my father was not impressed with what he had done. In fact, he had not thought to mention this portion of his life before that summer's conversation. Only when he recalled tales of his life on the ranch with my mother did he blurt it out. Like so many of my interviews for this book, I am initially taken aback by the lack of significance my interviewees feel about revealing their stories. My father spoke of his contact with former braceros while on the ranch:

> . . . *my foreman gave me orders in the morning to tell the braceros what to do and where to go and everything, he was really nice. I didn't have any problems with him, he even had co-workers say, you know the ones that used to live in the ranch before me. I learned a lot from these people (braceros who worked on the ranch), because I didn't know how to do nothing. They showed me how to build the barbed wire fences and all kinds of fences for the cattle and how to fix them and they showed me how to drive the bulldozers, trucks, and all the heavy equipment that was all over the ranch. . . .*
>
> (Interviewed with Benny López 2003)

As the front cover of the book reveals, my father and my uncle (paternal) had jobs associated with the Bracero Program. My uncle, in fact, used to drive the trucks shown in the book cover photo from the downtown section of Santa Barbara to the ranch each morning. Unfortunately, my uncle passed away before I could document his involvement with the program. My older brother recalls my father taking him down to the bracero camp and having him get haircuts from the bracero who used to cut the hair of other braceros. My older sister also recalled the kids who lived on the ranch who she played with while not at school. In short, the stories from my parents' past reflect how integrating the former Bracero Program was to Mexican American families.

Family Ties and the U.S. Mexican Bracero Program

The immigrant guest workers on the ranch where my father worked were Mexican braceros. Braceros (the term braceros in English means forearms) were immigrant guest workers from

Mexico who were contracted through the Mexico-U.S. Bracero Program (1942-1964). The former immigrant guest worker program, as I have learned through this study, played a vital role in the lives of many (Mexican) American families.

Indeed, not only have I learned about my own family's history, but also I have come to learn of other (Mexican) American families' involvement with the former Bracero Program. I met potential interviewees through some of my initial presentations (whether in my Chicano Studies classes or at professional conferences). Some of the oral histories in this book are from individuals whose fathers or grandfathers participated in the program.

This book has two stories to tell. First, are the stories of the families who became involved with the Bracero Program through the lives of former braceros. It's an *American* story that has yet to be fully told. I, like many other Chicano kids of my era, was living at a time when Mexican immigrants played a vital role toward the billion dollar agricultural industry. Attending a local Catholic grammar school in Santa Barbara, I was like any other Chicano kid who enjoyed playing freeze tag. As I played and went to school with my elementary friends, I did not know that some of them had fathers or parents who had arrived in the United States through the Bracero Program and that I would one day write their stories. Indeed, my best friend's dad[4] was a former bracero who later became very entrepreneurial buying local property and revitalizing them into rentals.

The second story is the larger issue of settlement by former braceros in the United States. Although originally intended to be a program for the recruitment of temporary guest workers, the legacy of the former guest worker program is of the families now permanently settled in the United States. Since its demise in 1964 the post-effects of the Bracero Program have been documented several times over (Garlarza, 1964; Driscoll, 1999; Calavita, 1992; Craig, 1971). However, the former braceros, now in their twilight years, are among those who best can speak of their experiences. Few, if any, first-person stories of braceros exist in this format. I wish to present their stories through their oral histories. The personal stories reveal their recruitment, work history, and their settlement. The stories from my oral histories have come from my students whose grandparents were former braceros. Every semester when I present my research on the former program I will have a student(s) who will tell me of their family ties to the former program.

We learn from their stories that guest workers are not temporary workers. As sociological studies have revealed, there is nothing temporary about guest workers. Rather, guest worker programs become the instrument for the permanent settlement of migrants (Briggs, 2004; Martin, 1998; Massey and Liang, 1989). Research has documented that former braceros simply did not return to Mexico following the end of the program. On the contrary, former braceros used their time in the United States to make repeated returns. Among those who stayed over, or simply crossed over illegally, were the ones who had established social connections. Beyond the economic benefits from crossing over, the reality of social relations established as former guest workers become too hard to overcome. Scholars have argued that the

---

[4] My best fried's father passed away before I could interview him for this book.

rise in the number of Mexicans who continued to migrate from Mexico in the late 1960s were former Mexican braceros (Baustista-Hayes, 2003; Bustamante, 1977).

Former Braceros Today

Since 1964, and the ending of the Bracero Program, many of those former braceros ensured that migration from Mexico continued well after the program's demise. Some former braceros legalized their status during the programs' existence, while others came as undocumented immigrants until they legalized their residency. In short, the Bracero Program continued to lay down the path for post-bracero migration and the migration that was to follow. There is no estimate of how many former braceros are currently living in the United States today, but I would venture to guess in the hundreds of thousands. Spread out in various states in the United States they have become a permanent fixture as settlers. They range in age from their late fifties to their early nineties. Some continue to remain in contact with relatives still in Mexico, but for the most part many of them have families of their own in the United States.

I began to consider what the former braceros might be doing today. How many were still around to interview? How would they discuss their time in the United States as former guest workers? Had enough research been conducted on the actual participants of the program? These questions become even more profound as the national discussion about documented and undocumented immigration from Mexico remains an important public policy issue. Indeed, almost every American president since the end of the Bracero Program has battled over the number of immigrants received annually from Mexico. President Bush's 2007 State of the Union addressed the idea of a guest worker program to help solve the immigration debate. Current and future projections of Mexican immigration suggest additional migration will occur. Based upon demographic projections in Mexico, where the largest population surge is currently among those under five years old, it appears that migration will continue for the foreseeable future, especially if the economic fortunes of Mexico does not radically change in creating a substantial middle class (Castaneda, 2008).

My book argues that the former Bracero Program served as an initial pathway for the former guest workers to develop social ties that would lead to their return migration to the United States following the program's demise. But more importantly, the book allows those who lived the experience of being immigrant guest workers to tell their stories through first-person accounts. Now in their golden years, these former braceros can speak to the issues they confronted while migrating north. In short, the migration of braceros did not end in 1964. Rather, the former Bracero Program laid the initial foundation for further migration from Mexico.

Now, as aging former guest workers in the United States, the question becomes not of what do with these former workers, rather it gives us insight into the process of settlement. The children of former braceros are now permanently working and living in the United States, and the grandchildren of former braceros are now entering into their young adult lives. The ties between Mexico and the United States remain. Contemporary anti-immigrant advocates do not recognize that migration is not only what occurred along the border just a day ago or a year ago. Rather, migration is a long-term phenomenon. A *New York Times* (2005) article on aging Mexican immigrants reveals the extent of how migration played out for those who used migration as a means of survival and have to decide their future as former migrants:

> *In 2003, an estimated 710,000 Mexicans over 60 lived in the United States, 63 percent more than a decade earlier, the National Population Council of Mexico concluded, based on Census Bureau figures.*
>
> (Mexicans at Home Abroad, 2005)

Increased border patrols and the perils of desert crossings have contributed to the numbers of illegal immigrants who no longer make repeated trips back and forth to Mexico. As wives and children have joined them in the United States, these aging immigrants become more settled in their new land.

This book examines how these former braceros became permanent settlers. By further examining their stories, we can also gain insight into the migration process and its long term consequences. As of this writing, the Bracero Program ended forty-four years ago. However, it remains relevant to the discussion on Mexican immigration policy settlement.

Theoretical Overview

"Common sense" explanations for the migration north of Mexican immigrants to the United States are offered daily by media pundits and public policy advocates. The wage differential between the United States and Mexico allow Mexicans to earn seven to ten times more than they could in Mexico (Massey, Durand, and Malone, 2003). Discussion on the topic of immigration has been examined from theories best known to explain its origins. The theories range from individual to broad-based explanations. Each theory attempts to offer plausible explanations of why immigrants suddenly move thousands of miles. In the case of Mexican immigration, Mexicans have a long history of migration back and forth from Mexico to the United States (Samora, 1971; Gonzalez, 2009; Cardoso, 1980). Beginning with the individual explanation, or neoclassical theory, social scientists have argued that Mexican immigration can be explained from a cost-benefits decision. The neoclassical or push-pull theory of migration argues that migrants simply weigh the difference between the cost and the benefits of migration. The cost factors include the possibility of being apprehended crossing the border, while leaving their family and familiar surroundings behind. The benefit factor is the higher wages immigrants can earn in the new host country and return to family in Mexico (Borjas, 1989; Chiswick, 1999).

Everyday explanations for migration from Mexico do not account for the complexity of migration. As we have seen, those who have used migration as a means to overcome economic problems in their country of origin are not always the poorest. Portes and Rumbaut (2006) have argued that potential migrants are more likely to come from working or middle class backgrounds. The expense for migrating can be quite costly. The cost of migrations for undocumented can be in the thousands of dollars to pay for a "coyote" or smuggler.

Critics of this theory insist it is short sighted and does not incorporate enough of the "bigger picture" issues involving the migration experience. Individual migrants make decisions to cross the border, knowing that getting caught is highly probable. However, migration is more than an individual act; it involves many elements or stages. International migration is a much broader phenomenon. The "pioneering" migrant takes all the initial risks involved during the first couple of trips. However, after repeated trips the migrant is likely to expand his contacts and gain valuable experience in the host country. Once migrants have developed repeated routes, they will find themselves involved in a host of social relationships. After their initial migration the circle of potential migrants begins to include family members, friends, and perhaps eventually members of the communities they are migrating from (Massey and Durand, 2004; Levitt and Waters, 2002).

Shortfalls in the explanations offered by neoclassical theory have made it difficult to rely upon a cost-benefits view. While neoclassical theorists offer a higher wage differential as the basis for migration, it does not explain why migrants will choose to drop out of the labor market and return to Mexico. It would appear that migration has many more social consequences that neoclassical theorists can't account for. In short, international migration entails a broader view and shows how migrants are able to sustain repeated migration.

Rather than simply describe migration as a cost-benefits decision, recent theories emphasize the role that families, social networks, and other structural conditions for stimulating migration (Corneluis, 1981; Massey, 1987; Massey and Durand, 2004). Other theories employed to explain international migration are dual economy, world systems, and social capital theory. The dual economy theory argues that low wage laborers are recruited to enter secondary sector employment. The dual economy model divides the labor market into primary and secondary sectors. Primary sectors are said to employ unionized, professional workers through contracts. Secondary sector workers are poorly paid, have a high rate of turn over, and are more likely to experience harsh working conditions (Piore, 1979). Immigrants are recruited to fill jobs that most native-born workers reject. According to economist Michael Piore (1979), immigrants play an important role by supplementing the labor market. In short, dual economy theory explains why immigrants can be found employed in the worst occupations (secondary sectors) and are often the last hired and first fired. High turn over rates occur more often in secondary sector occupations.

The World System theory argues that immigrants tend to migrate from semi-periphery countries to core countries in order to fill secondary employment opportunities (Acuna, 2007). Displacement of workers occurs in semi-periphery countries such as Mexico and the incentive to migrate to more advanced countries such as the United States becomes viable as a means of economic survival (Valdes, 2000). Mexico is a developing nation. The United States is a highly advanced country and relies more upon a knowledge-based economy (Sassen, 2006). Service-sectors jobs are abundant. High-end and low-end service jobs grow and workers are needed to fill both sectors. At the high end are workers with professional skills and advanced education. Low-end workers are less skilled, with few educational credentials, and are more likely employed in dead-end jobs. Mexican immigrants are employed in the low-end jobs as domestics, dishwashers, gardeners, and custodians. With Mexico's surplus of workers and proximity to the border, workers are easily recruited to the United States to fill low-end jobs.

Migration occurs under conditions that create multiple social mechanisms that operate to get migrants into the migration stream (Massy, Durand, and Malone, 2003). Indeed, as migration occurs more frequently after the initial migration, the cost of future migration is reduced. Migrants are able to rely upon pioneers who paved the way for others to follow. The buildup of social networks creates opportunities not only for new immigrants, but also for multiple return migrations (Aguilera and Massey, 2003). One theory that argues a broader perspective is the social capital theory. Constructed from the work of Pierre Bourdie (1986), this theory claims that social relations are developed through investment strategies which allow for cultural and economic returns. Unable to finance the cost of migrating abroad, social capital theory argues that migrants earn social capital through social networks. Social networks serve migrants as a means of providing information about jobs and wages in the United States (Aguilera and Massey, 2003; Aguilera, 2002). Social capital helps to lower the cost to migrants who increase their wages and ensure their employment opportunities (Massey, Alarcon, Durand, and Gonzalez, 1987).

Immigration scholars have examined the former Bracero Program employing the social capital theory (Massey and Liang, 1989). The experience of braceros was not only contracting an initial agreement, but many renewed their contracts. Employers were often very grateful for the work ethic braceros exemplified with their ability to endure some of the harshest working conditions. When the contracts would come to an end, employers often encouraged them to renew their contracts without losing contact with them. Some went as far as "jumping" their contracts with the encouragement of their employers. The development of social networks led braceros to establish permanency in the United States.

Many braceros had to leave families behind in Mexico, which often meant enduring dual lives. Sending money home to wives and children created and maintained a dual existence on both sides of the border. If unmarried, some braceros also had to help their parents with money to maintain their family farms. Multiple renewals of contracts and increased movement back and forth from Mexico led to the decision to remain in the United States. Even after completing their contracts, former braceros would secure their legal residence or simply migrate as undocumented immigrants. Many years following their initial bracero experience, former braceros would use their prior knowledge of job opportunities and cultural familiarity with the United States in order to perpetuate their continual migration north.

Research Design and Methodology

The focus of the book is to examine how former braceros came initially as immigrant guest workers and eventually settled in the United States. The site of the project began in Santa Barbara (as previously recounted by the discussion between my parents). I conducted interviews in the following California cities: San Jose, Los Angeles, Buttonwillow, Carpentaria, Goleta, Guadalupe, Santa Maria, Oxnard, and many others. In total, I have conducted fifty interviews to date.[5]

---

[5] When time and money permit, I continue to interview former braceros; because of their current age, many stories would be lost. I should also note that the Smithsonian Institute and the Oral History Institute at the University of Texas, El Paso have been conducting town hall meetings to ensure the stories of former braceros are preserved.

This study of Mexican braceros employed qualitative research methods. Through in-depth interviews, former braceros were interviewed regarding their recruitment, transportation, housing, employment, and later settlement in the United States. To conduct the interviews, a snowball sampling technique was used to contact braceros. The first contacted was through my father's friendship with a former bracero. The friendship began as my father worked alongside the braceros at the ranch my dad worked for ten years. Over the years their friendship has been maintained by phone calls and visits to my parents' home. Ultimately, the friendship was strengthened by my father becoming *compadres* with the bracero. The first interview began in December of 2001. I was able to contact other former braceros from that first interview.

The method for the interviews was semi-structured. Because former braceros are not confined to one city or region, it was up to me to seek out their whereabouts. My first interview was with one of my father's co-workers on the ranch. Working on the ranch together for many years, they formed a friendship that lasted well beyond their time on the ranch. I recall my father's friend appearing at our house on various occasions to speak to my father. My father encouraged him to bring his family from Mexico to settle here. Employing a series of questions, I conducted what would be two to three hour interviews with each former bracero. Most of the interviews were conducted at their homes. With only a few exceptions all the interviews were conducted in Spanish. The interviews have been subsequently translated into English by students who I have employed. Sometimes the interviews included other family members, such as the bracero wives and sometimes their children. This was the first opportunity for some of the children of these former braceros to hear the stories of their fathers' experience as braceros. Most of the children of these former braceros are now reaching middle age.

From my initial interview I was able to contact additional braceros to interview. I also found additional contacts through some unexpected sources. As a Chicano Studies professor I come into contact with students and other scholars. Through courses in Chicano Studies, I have discussed my research project and given lectures to discuss the importance of the program. Not a semester goes by that one or more students will let me know of a family member who was involved with the program. Additionally, I have presented my research on the former Bracero Program at conferences or other venues, and I continue to come in contact with others whose family members have been involved with the program. Knowing that my research has connected so many people has made this project that more exciting and important to document the former braceros involvement.

Additional contacts were through presentations at community organizations. Among the organizations I was able to present my study to were the Santa Barbara Hispanic Chamber, the Casa de la Raza (in Santa Barbara), the National Association of Chicana and Chicano Studies annual meetings, and the Pacifica Sociological Association annual meetings. I also attended various bracero meetings held in Los Angeles, Salinas, Santa Maria, and Watsonville.

Although limited to various cities in California, the former braceros interviewed worked in the states of Arizona, Texas, Illinois, Wisconsin, Arkansas, Missouri, Washington, Oregon, Idaho, Pennsylvania, Michigan, and other states. As diverse as the locations where these former braceros worked, so was their years of participation in the program. Indeed some of the braceros I interviewed were among the earliest participants (1942) and others were at the end of the program's demise (1964). As of this writing of the book, I continue to interview former braceros. The age of these former braceros range between those in their late fifties and those as old as their early eighties. I will likely continue to interview former braceros even after the completion of the book. I believe that it is important to preserve as many of these stories as possible.

One of the reasons I feel compelled to continue to document their lives is the continued need for labor in the agricultural sector of the U.S. economy. Labor shortages, whether perceived or in truth real, will likely be filled by immigrants rather than native-born Americans. The continued argument in favor of another guest worker program continues to be debated among politicians, growers, and anti-immigrant advocates. Without an understanding of the historical guest worker programs, the lives of the potential workers will be in jeopardy by repeating the errors of the past.

Perhaps one of the most interesting aspects of the interview process was finding out that I had grown up with some of the children of these former braceros. In one case, I learned that I had worked with one of the braceros I interviewed during my part-time job as a parking lot attendant while attending a local college. As a child I attended a Catholic grammar school. Many of the children who attended the school were of Mexican-origin. I can now understand how a handful of the students did poorly, since many of their family members were making the immigrant transition to American life. I realize even more that my (peer) class was not the only one affected by the Bracero Program. Many students who attended the same grammar school before me and after were children of former braceros. It wasn't until I began locating the former braceros that I became aware of the extent that the program had reached into other families in the area.

The experience of interviewing these former braceros has been quite rewarding. It's taken me back to my youth and caused me to realize how my childhood friends must have had difficulties adjusting to life in Santa Barbara. So the book has not only been a story of braceros, but also a personal reflection on those with whom I grew up. In short, this is an American story—a multi-generational American story of settlement in the United States. Since 1964 (the end of the Bracero Program), the story repeats itself every time a new set of migrants establish themselves initially as workers and later as entire families.

Conclusion

This book-length study of the former guest workers creates the opportunity to hear from those who actively participated in the program. Other studies have already done an analysis of the former Bracero Program, but few studies have focused on the oral histories of these former guest workers. Who is better prepared to explain the problems associated with contemporary guest worker program proposals than the individuals who were previously employed in them?

The Introduction outlines the focus of the book and sets the analytical agenda for what will be the analysis of the book. Chapter One describes the history of the Bracero Program. Although the Bracero Program was the largest sustained guest worker program during the twentieth century, few people outside the Mexican American community know of its existence. Many people are aware of the undocumented immigrant "problem" facing the country, but fewer people know of the stimulated migration that the former Bracero Program created and maintained years after the program's demise. Chapter Two analyzes the recruitment process. Chapter Three examines the travel experiences of braceros and their eventual crossing of the U.S.-Mexico border. This chapter shows the treatment of braceros by doctors, train operators, and others who were the first line of contact many Mexicans had with officials from the United States. Chapter Four examines the field experience of former braceros, their living conditions, and finally their return migration to the border. Chapter Five reveals the factors for the settlement of Mexican braceros in the United States. Most of the braceros interviewed for this book have decided to remain in the United States rather than return to Mexico. Little prior information from the former braceros has documented the reasons for their settlement. Chapter Six discusses the renewed talks of a future bracero-like program. Indeed, I discuss concerns should another guest worker program develop.

CHAPTER 1

Mexican Immigration and the U.S.-Mexico Bracero Program

Well, when we came here the first time it was nice they treated us well, but after a while people started to discriminate and racism grew more. That's why a lot of people did not want to come anymore. People started to put up posters on the doors of their establishments that said, "No Mexicans allowed." But before that everything was okay, they treated us well. That was in 1956 or 1957, there was not a lot of racism, but it started to grow when a lot of braceros came. They would bring more people than what was necessary. Sometimes, some people would say that they had not worked all week, because there were not enough jobs. I do not know why they brought so many people if they were not going to have jobs for them. I guess they thought that they were going to need all of them, but if they did not have enough jobs for everybody they should not have contracted all those people.

(Quote from former bracero from his 1950s migration experience)

Below I describe two historical events which at first do not appear to have any connection to one another. However, both are important toward understanding the current migration experience of Mexican immigrants to the United States. The first event is the pro-immigration marches of the early twenty-first century. On May 1st of 2006, in one of the largest protests ever witnessed in the United States (and not since the 1960s Vietnam protests), millions of documented and undocumented Mexican and Latino immigrants hit the streets of U.S. cities around the country. The headlines in the *New York Times* (Archibold, 2006) the day after the

May 1st protest read, "*Immigrants Take to U.S. Streets in Show of Strength*." Indeed, the sheer volume of protesters was quite remarkable. However, due to Americans' stereotypes of immigrant passivity and fear, they were surprised to see so many undocumented immigrants involved in the protests.

The lives of undocumented immigrants in the United States tend to be hidden from the mainstream (Chavez, 1993). The daily experience of undocumented immigrants is their fear of being caught by the Immigration and Customs Enforcement (ICE) or being fired from their jobs if caught taking a sick day to engage in protests. The protests were in reaction to the proposed legislation Senate Bill HR 4437, where it would have made being an undocumented immigrant in the United States a felony. The legislation sponsored by Congressman James Sensenbrenner Jr. was proposed as a solution to the number of undocumented immigrants estimated to be around ten to twelve million. One of the major provisions of the legislation stated:

> "Unlawful presence" would now be considered a crime and a felony, meaning that undocumented immigrants may have to serve jail time and would be barred from future legal status and from re-entry into the country.

The second event occurred with the ending of the U.S.-Mexico Bracero Program. On January 1, 1964, one of the longest sustained guest worker programs of the twentieth century came to an end. After years of struggling to end what critics argued was legalized slavery, the U.S.-Mexico Bracero Program was formally ended. The U.S.-Mexico Bracero Program (1942-1964) marked a significant period of recruitment of Mexican immigrants to the United States during the twentieth century (Garcia, 1982; Massey, Jorge Durand, and Nolan J. Malone, 2002; Garlarza, 1964; Samora, 1971; Driscoll, 1999). Indeed, the history of the twentieth century is marked by episodes of immigration from Mexico, and the legacy of the Bracero Program is an important era in light of its impact upon contemporary immigration issues (Massey and Durand, 2002; Martinez, 2000).

Current debates on immigration reform include a proposal for yet another guest worker program (Malkin, 2007). Resurrecting a similar guest worker program such as the former U.S.-Mexico Bracero Program would invite similar "problems" associated with guest worker programs (Briggs, 2004). Abuses ranged from denying workers their wages, hazardous working conditions, deplorable housing, unpaid savings accounts, unsanitary food conditions, and denied entry to local restaurants (Garlarza, 1964; Driscoll, 1999; Gamboa, 1987; Calavita, 1992).

Although these two events are from different historical periods, they remain connected to one another. Immigration reform ties these events. Current and previous immigration reform has been a constant theme between the United States and Mexico. Whether the issue was labor shortages in the United States or labor surpluses in Mexico, the two issues contrasted the policies of what to do about Mexican (undocumented) immigration. Critics argue that the debate has favored United States' interests more so than Mexico's (Durand and Massey, 1992). The problem among employers is their desire to find an adequate supply of workers. Most American born workers do not want to do agricultural work. Working in the fields is physically demanding, pays low wages, and is seasonal. Immigrants seeking employment find working in the agricultural sector easily accessible. The opinion of many Americans is that agricultural work is for foreign workers (Massey, Durand, and Malone, 2002; Piore, 1979).

The last major piece of immigration reform was the *Immigration Reform and Control Act* of 1986 (IRCA). Supported by Ronald Regan and passed by the U.S. Congress, it gave millions of undocumented Mexican immigrants the opportunity to legalize their status. According to the legislation, if immigrants could prove that they entered the United States prior to January 1, 1982, they could earn permanent residence. Under IRCA legislation, 2.7 million undocumented immigrants legalized their status (Orrenius and Zavodny, 2005). Hoping to stem the tide of undocumented immigration with the passage of IRCA, the legislation's effect had mixed results. Indeed, Woodrow and Passel's (1990) study concluded that despite the legislation, undocumented immigrants continued to migrate. Other studies argued that although the level of undocumented immigrants lowered for the next few years, by the early 1990s the number of undocumented immigrants from Mexico began to surge once again (Massey, 2000). While other studies concluded that undocumented immigration lowered for a time after the legislation passage, according to Bean, Edmonston, and Passel's (1990) analysis, apprehensions declined 27 percent after ICRA. Lastly, White, Bean, and Espenshade's (1990) study also found similar results with lower declines in apprehensions.

Although Mexican immigrants have been migrating back and forth from Mexico and to the United States for generations now, there remain unsolved public policy approaches to this human phenomenon. According to sociologist Douglas Massey, the public policy approach to undocumented immigration throughout the twentieth century has been detrimental toward solving the problem. Massey argues that the United States continually contradicts what it supposedly wants to do. With the further integrating of the economies of Mexico, Canada, and the United States with the passage of NAFTA in 1994, undocumented immigration remains part of the consequences. Indeed, Massey (2007) argues in an editorial: *"Rather than slowing the inflow of undocumented migrants, this policy of insisting on separation of labor while promoting integration of trade has brought about an array of unintended negative consequences."*

In the end, U.S. policy has not decreased the number of undocumented crossings, but rather has diverted it from areas or regions along the border that no longer serve as major entry points. No longer are San Diego and El Paso the main entry points for Mexican immigrants such as during the Bracero Program. Rather, Mexican immigrants who continue to migrate use less patrolled regions of the border, such as rural Arizona, with sometimes dire consequences. Since the late 1980s, the number of deaths along the border has increased as Mexican immigrants have diverted their crossing to remote and more dangerous areas which can mean days without human contact or food and water. In a border study of the number of deaths in the United States among undocumented immigrants, Eschbach, Hagan, Rodriguez, Hernandez, and Bailey (1999) found that 200 to 330 deaths occur each year.

In an ironic twist of fate, today's immigration debate reminds us of the anti-Mexican hysteria of previous eras. Indeed, by the spring of 2006, undocumented Mexican immigrants were being vilified for being in the United States. Critics argued the anti-immigration response headed by the HR 4437 bill (Preston, 2006), would penalize immigrants even though sectors of the U.S. economy continues to rely on their labor (Valenzuela, 2001). The two contrasting views can't be ignored for their similarities. Despite the lapsed time, Mexican immigration can always be used to scapegoat the economic woes of the United States whether in the past or now in the new century.

New Directions in Chicano Social History

Unlike historical studies that examine the lives of humans from the top down, this book attempts to examine previous events from the bottom up (Zinn, 1996). Although I do not claim to be a historian, since my degree is in sociology, I do wish to argue that I am contributing to the ever-developing field of Chicano Studies. In some small way, I want to extend the work of those who came before me. One of my mentors at the beginning of my academic career was Dr. Julian Samora. Through Dr. Samora's mentorship I was given increased insight into the experience of Mexican immigrants and their hardships. Arguably, Dr. Samora is a pioneer in the field of Chicano Studies (Pulido, Driscoll De Alvarado, and Samora, 2009). His legacy continues to lay the foundation for how scholars approach the field of Mexican immigration. I can only hope to bring justice to his legacy by adding to the discourse on Mexican immigration. His book, *Los Mojados: The Wetback Story* (1971), continues to be cited by scholars for his ground-breaking examination of undocumented immigration. My examination of Mexican braceros is hopefully a continuation of that legacy of how former braceros are now settled in the United States as permanent residents.

In a recent publication, Chicana and Chicano historians and social scientists (Rochin and Valdes, 2000) addressed the following question: What is the past, present, and future direction of Chicana/o history? Through a series of original articles written by Chicana and Chicano scholars (in some cases through their own stories), they address the interdisciplinary development of Chicana/o history. It is my hope that this book will reflect the legacy of Chicana/o scholarship that remains uncovered and is crucial to explain the contributions of Mexican-origin people to the United States.

Indeed, the history of Chicanas and Chicanos in the United States needs to be told. So much of the history of Chicanas and Chicanos in the United States remains untold and those stories are unfolding. Since 1848 (and before) the development of Chicano communities in the United States was a part of the historical development of the Southwest and Midwest (Acuna, 2006; McWilliams, 1948). Now, due to increased immigration and high fertility rates, a noticeable number of people of Mexican origin can be found in all fifty states. Despite the void, Chicana and Chicano historians have increased from their marginal positions during the 1960s and 1970s toward occupying important positions within the academy. Among the top Chicana and Chicano scholars today (not a conclusive list) are Dr. George Sanchez, Dr. Dominic Valdez, Dr. Vick Ruiz, Dr. Denise Segura, and others, whose legacies are indebted to the likes of Dr. Julian Samora, Dr. Ernesto Garlarza, and Ms. Betita Martinez. However, much work needs to be done in the form of increased presence of Chicana and Chicano scholars in order to ensure that new strands of scholarship aimed at telling the historical contributions of Mexican-origin people in the United States.

Much of the work from the 1960s and 1970s was based upon the pioneering work of former scholars such as Dr. Julian Samora, a professor of sociology and anthropology at the University of Notre Dame. Dr. Samora along with graduate students Dr. Jorge Bustamante and Dr. Gilberto Cardenas published the seminal book *Los Mojados: The Wetback Story*, which remains an important contribution to the migration history of Mexican immigrants to the United

States. Also, scholar/activist Dr. Ernesto Garlarza was a major influence upon the research of Mexican-origin people in the United States. One of Dr. Garlarza's most important contributions was his pivotal study on U.S.-Mexico Bracero Program. His book, *Merchants of Labor: The Mexican Bracero Story* is a classic. The books and essays on Chicano folklore by Ms. Jovita Gonzalez Mireles are also very timely for their contributions. Chicana and Chicano scholars continue to need to pay homage to these pioneering scholars in the field of Chicano Studies. They were working in the field of Chicano Studies before there was a discipline of Chicano Studies (Rochin and Valdes, 2000; Martinez, 1999).

Although the historical relationship between Mexico and the United States has been told many times before, it wasn't until the past few decades that Chicana/o historians have uncovered the contributions of Mexican immigrants to the industrial development of the Southwest and Midwest during the twentieth century. Much of the initial studies were historical accounts of Mexican immigrants finding opportunities in the north.

For example, Chicano historians have written on the enormous contributions of Mexican laborers during the early twentieth century. Zaragosa Vargas has written on the migration of Mexican laborers to the Midwest. In his book (1993), *Proletarians of the North: A History of Mexican Industrial Workers in Detroit and the Midwest, 1917-1933*, Vargas documented the recruitment of Mexican laborers to the industrial Midwest. According to Vargas, Mexican immigrants were part of the industrial buildup of manufacturing jobs related to the steel, auto, and oil industries. Contributing to the understanding of Mexican immigrant settlement in the Midwest, a groundbreaking work is that of Dennis Nodin Valdes. Valdes' book (2000), *Barrios Nortenos: St. Paul and Midwestern Mexican Communities in the Twentieth Century* argues that Mexican immigrants have a long history of settlement in the Midwest. Without the research of Vargas or Valdes, little of the economic contributions of Mexican immigrants in the industrial Midwest would be known. Chicano historian Mario T. Garcia's book (1981), *Desert Immigrants; The Mexicans of El Paso, 1880-1920*, documented the account of Mexican immigrants to the Southwest from the late nineteenth century and early twentieth century. Garcia's book recounts the migration of Mexican immigrants across the Southwest during the period of Mexico's economic instability. Next, Manuel Gamio's (1930) *Mexican Immigration to the United States: An Autobiography* is a classic account of Mexican immigration in the early twentieth century. Gamio's pioneering work continues to guide current scholars for its effort to document first-person accounts of Mexican immigrants.

Lawrence Cardoso's (1980), *Mexican Emigration to the United States, 1897-1930: Socio-Economic Patterns*, historical account of the migration of Mexicans to the United States is a valuable source for understanding the transnational connection of the United States and Mexico. Not only were Mexican immigrants migrating to the Southwest, Cardoso also points to the increased number of Mexicans to the Midwest. Without these groundbreaking accounts, most of the historical knowledge of the importance of Mexican immigrants during this period would remain complicated.

Chicana scholars have increased in recent years and their work has contributed to the knowledge of Mexican women and their role as mothers and also as providers. Chicana historian Vicki Ruiz (2008) tells of the life of Mexican women in the twentieth century. In her book,

From Out of the Shadows: Mexican Women in the Twentieth-Century America, she details through oral histories the work of Mexican women in unions, auxiliaries, and the civil rights movement. Despite their gender status, Ruiz illuminates the positive inroads that Mexican women had on the development of the Southwest through their activism. Other Chicana historians such as Deana Gonzalez, Lorena Oropeza, Cynthia Orozco, and Camille Guerin Gonzales contributed to the understanding of Chicana/o history.

The body of Chicana/o history reveals the inroads toward important historical eras often ignored by mainstream historians. Chicana/o history employs a different view of the events that have transpired from the time in which Chicana/os became part of the United States when the war between Mexico and the United States concluded in 1848. Since 1848, Chicana/os have been major contributors to the development of the Southwest, Midwest and, now of course, the entire nation. But it is shortsighted to assume the role of Chicanas/os as secondary characters in the American drama. Indeed, Chicanas/os have played significant roles. One aspect of their roles involved their participation in the U.S.-Mexico Bracero Program. Little in the way of historical documentation or recognition regarding the role that Mexican immigrants played during the era of the Bracero Program is mentioned beyond academic circles. Only within the last few years has the historical contribution of Mexican braceros become a national concern as the Smithsonian and the Oral History Institute at the University of Texas, El Paso began collecting oral histories. Through the use of town hall meetings both institutions are collecting stories of former Mexican braceros before they are lost forever. It is crucial that future generations of Americans understand the importance of the former U.S-Mexico Bracero Program.

The history of America is a multicultural history. Within that same vein, migration history is the story of the United States. Americans lacking a historical perspective of Mexican immigration are rendering themselves ill informed on an important part of their past; this creates a problem for understanding the present and future of Mexican immigration to the United States. All future demographic projections suggest continued migration from Mexico despite attempts to limit or block immigrants from crossing the U.S-Mexico border. A viable solution based on logical or humane efforts to understand its importance for both sides will dictate how we as a nation face this issue.

The lives of former Mexican braceros are not just an abstract concept to be included as an afterthought. Rather a first-hand account provides rich detail to their experiences as former guest workers. Who better to tell the stories of how former guest workers were treated in the United States than those who actually participated in the program? From these stories readers will see how guest worker programs are plagued with inherent problems. At best, readers will get insights into a program that has carried on with the settlement of many of the former guest workers now in the United States. A renewed guest worker program would also carry with it similar issues many Americans will not confront until years later. Do Americans want increased settlement of former guest workers should a new program be devised? If not, then a sobering examination of just how the post-effects of a guest worker program would emerge now rather than years later.

History of Mexican Immigration to the United States

Central to the discussion of the former U.S.-Mexico Bracero Program is the history of recruitment to, and settlement in, the United States of Mexican immigrants. Indeed much of the twentieth century was about the migration of Mexicans to the United States. Like my sociological predecessors, I will examine the historical migration of Mexican immigration through the following eras: the *Classical Era*, the *Bracero Era*, the *Post-Bracero Era*, and finally the *Post-IRCA era* (Durand, Massey, and Charvet, 2000).

Each period of the history of immigration from Mexico marks different eras, but several themes remain constant throughout. Mexican immigrants have been migrating back and forth for many centuries. Recruitment of documented and undocumented immigrants from Mexico is consistent with U.S.-Mexico relations. The 2,000 mile border between Mexico and the United States is unique and is unlike any other border region. The United States is an advanced society economically and Mexico is a developing country. There is a growing middle class in Mexico. The middle class in the United States is still the majority, but has been experiencing a downward movement economically. The racial divide in both countries affects how race relations are determined and who remains on top of the racial hierarchy. People of Mexican origin in the United States face a history of racial strife that is consistent with other racial groups battle for equality.[1] People of Mexican origin have been recruited for their labor for many decades and like other prior immigrant groups are racially and ethnically diverse. English is not always their primary language, especially among first-generation Mexican immigrants. And finally, Mexican immigration and the historical settlement of Mexican-origin people in the United States is one that will continue well into this current century.

Classical Era

After the end of the U.S.-Mexico war in 1848, only a "handful" of Mexicans were left behind in the U.S occupied territory. It is estimated that only about 500,000 Mexicans decided to stay in the United States following the war (Samora, 1975; Samora, 1971; Cardoso, 1980). Although there were accounts of Mexicans crossing over the border to the United States, it was not until the first decades of the twentieth century that migration across the Mexican border became a public policy priority. Following the loss of half of Mexico's former northern territory, the Mexicans who remained in the Southwest soon found their lives transformed. According to various studies, the racial hierarchy established toward Mexicans by Anglos was to enforce an inferior status (De Leon, 1983; Almaguer, 2008). Former landowners among the Mexican population were turned into proletarians as land was stolen or simply violently taken (Barrera, 1979, Acuna, 2007). In short, the first decades following the loss of the Southwest

---

[1] However, unlike previous immigrant groups, Mexicans continue to have a close proximity to the United States, are still recruited as immigrant labor, and have treaty rights since the signing of the Treaty of Guadalupe-Hildago back in 1948.

paved the way for intolerance toward Mexicans well into the late nineteenth century and continued into the next century.

On the Mexican side of the border, with the presidency of Mexico in the hands of Porfirio Diaz (1876-1910), migration of Mexicans to the United States escalated. For thirty-five years President Diaz ruled Mexico with an iron fist. Political rivals could not voice their opposition to Diaz for fear of political reprisals. Known as the *Porfiriato*, Diaz allowed foreign investors access to Mexico's industrial sector. Wanting to modernize Mexico, Diaz looked toward improving Mexico's industrial sectors, which included its railroads, mines, and oil industries. Indeed, evidence of the development of Mexico's infrastructure was the construction of Mexico's railroad lines. In 1892, there were only 6,876 lines of railroad. By 1910, the number of railroad lines in Mexico had increased to 12,000 miles. Despite the progress in the development of Mexico's industrialization process, it came at a human price.

Mexico's economic instability, particularly in the rural regions, made it virtually impossible for peasant workers to find enough land to feed themselves and their families. Forced from their traditional ties to *ejidos* (communal farm lands) many peasants escaped the poverty of rural living in favor of urban life. However, with the instability of the peso due to the foreign dominance of the Mexican economy by companies from United States, Great Britain, and France, revolution became the only alternative to the economic policies of Diaz. In addition, the increasing population growth due to the lowering of infant mortality rates because of improved health care led many Mexicans to consider "temporary" migration north.[2]

By 1910, the blood of Mexicans was being spilled in favor of land and liberty. What started as a simple protest by Francisco I. Madero led to the uprising of Mexico's elites. Madero protested what he believed was a rigged presidential election (Gonzales, 2000). Within three months following his rise to power, Madero was assassinated. Revolution brought with it chaos in Mexico. Ordinary Mexicans were caught between those fighting against the Diaz regime and those who were supporting the fight for land and liberty. Revolutionary leaders such as Emiliano Zapata and Pancho Villa led various sections of Mexico's insurgents. In the South, Zapata headed forces against Diaz, and in the North Villa fought against Diaz and the U.S. forces attempting to capture him. Others, such as the Flores Magon brothers, questioned the overthrow of the Diaz regime. By 1906, the Magon brothers instigated a series of rebellions in Northern Mexico. Ultimately, the Magon brothers sought refuge in the United States, first in San Antonio, Texas, next in St. Louis, Missouri, and then later in Los Angeles, California. Not until the presidency of Alvaro Obregon did political stability occur in Mexico. However, the demand of land reform was not solved despite many lives lost during the Mexican Revolution. The discontent escalated with the Cristero Rebellion (1926-1929) which propelled Francisco I. Madero to the Presidency of Mexico. Despite the presidential changes, many of the challenges affecting the peasantry remained unmet. Unemployed Mexicans unable to find steady work used migration as a means of survival. Ten percent of Mexico's population crossed over to the United States.

---

[2] The migration of Mexican immigrants in the early twentieth century was to be temporary, similar to the intentions proposed later for the support of the U.S.-Mexico Bracero Program.

On the U.S side, the demand for labor from Mexico increased. Policies restricting immigration from Asia and Europe had an effect. The Chinese were the first group to feel the sting of immigration restrictions. In 1882, the Chinese Exclusion Act prevented further immigration from China. By the turn of the century, Chinese immigration had dwindled to a leaky few. Among other groups from Asia, Japanese and Filipino workers who had been first recruited to the United States to fill agricultural shortages were restricted with the passage of the Gentlemen's Agreement Act of 1908. Lured to work in such states as Hawaii and California, ever-increasing resentment toward Japanese and Filipinos led to further immigration restrictions.

Similar anti-immigrant sentiment was targeted toward Southern and Eastern immigrants as the United States entered into World War I. Fearing Southern and Eastern immigrants would side with the enemy, immigration restrictions ensued with the passage of the *1917 Immigration Act*. The *1917 Act* was best known for setting quotas. Limiting the number of these former immigrant groups into the United States created a gap in labor within the Southwest and the Midwest (Valdes, 2000). Besides quotas, immigrants from non-Western countries also faced literacy exams and a head tax.[3]

In California, as the demand for fresh fruits and vegetables increased, agricultural growers turned toward the U.S. government for help. Recruitment of Mexican workers resulted with American recruiters entering Mexico with offers of work. As restrictions increased towards other immigrant groups, Mexican immigrants were given exemptions. Exemptions meant Mexican immigrants did not have to pay fees or pass literacy exams. The period from 1900 to 1929 was labeled as *El Enganche*. Translated literally, the term *el enganche* means the "hook." Using the railroads as the means to gain access into Mexico, private recruiters crossed the U.S.-Mexico border. According to American growers, Mexican workers were preferred as they *knew their place* (Kiser and Silverman, 1973). In short, the stereotype of Mexican workers as docile and willing to endure harsh conditions would later come back to haunt American employers (McWilliams, 1948).

Lured by higher wages and paid transportation, Mexican workers took the bait. Once in the United States, they learned that recruiters had lied. Working conditions were worse than promised, wages were lower than initially offered, and they found themselves paying higher interest rates on the cost of things sold to them by company stores. Indebted, they soon discovered that they were indentured to their employers (Garcia 1981).

Despite the obvious hardships endured by many Mexican immigrants, the number of migrants continued to increase. Not only did they work in the agricultural sectors picking cotton, harvesting sugar beets, picking tomatoes, but they also found their ways toward other industries. In the Midwest, the opportunity to work in industries repairing railroads, building automobiles, meat-packing, and working in the steel industry were available to Mexican immigrants (Vargas, 2002; Martinez, 2000). With the outbreak of World War I, the pursuit of

---

[3] German foreign secretary Arthur Zimmerman (1958) sought an alliance between Germany and Mexico suggesting Mexico invade the United States from the south. In return, Mexico would get back the land lost to the United States following the conclusion of the war between Mexico and the United States in 1848. The United States would soon enter into World War I following the Zimmerman's telegram discovery by U.S. authorities.

Mexican workers accelerated. The U.S. government directly recruited Mexicans and it lasted until the end of the war. Soon, with the dark cloud of economic depression in the late 1920s, Mexican immigrants no longer looked quite so lucrative to recruit. Anti-Mexican sentiment grew as the unemployment rate of Anglos rose as the economic fortunes of the United States began to directly affect certain sectors of the economy. By the early 1930s, anti-Mexican sentiment reached a fever pitch. Part of the anti-Mexican resentment was based on strike activities by Mexican workers in the melon, berry, sugar beet, and mining industries throughout the Southwest and Midwest (Valdez, 2000). The myth that Mexican immigrants were docile or content with their "lot" as poor working class immigrants was brought to light with Mexican immigrants forming unions (McWilliams, 1975, Acuna, 2007). In the mining camps of Clifton, Morenci, and Metclalf, Mexican strikers were rounded up and deported by boxcars and dumped in the open desert without food or water.

The decade of the 1930s was a dark era for Chicanos and Mexican immigrants. Chicanos and Mexican immigrants and their cultural differences reminded Anglos of the differences found among Chinese and Japanese. Asians had been targeted for exclusion and quotas to keep their population numbers down. With the Border Patrol becoming a governmental agency to enforce unwanted immigrants in 1924, Chinese immigrants were targeted for their undocumented migration from the Mexican and Canadian borders. Chinese immigrants at the Mexican border attempted to cross by dressing similar to Mexicans. The *Exclusion Act* of 1882 stripped some Chinese of their citizenship. The Japanese immigrant experience was no better than that of the Chinese. After being recruited to Hawaii and California, the resentment toward the Japanese began as they were entrepreneurial in acquiring farm land. Resourceful as laborers, they were even better as farm owners. In California, the Japanese reclaimed waste lands and made them profitable. By the early 1940s, Japanese farmers dominated the cultivation of celery, strawberries, lettuce, asparagus, and many other fruits and vegetables in California.

Although previous decades saw the recruitment of Mexican immigrants to the United States, it was short-lived. The economic crisis to the U.S. economy, also known as the Great Depression, introduced a new era between Mexico and the United States. Rising unemployment among Americans caused deep resentment. Part of the response toward the economic ills facing many Anglos was to consider deporting Mexican immigrants. Indeed, the rights of Chicanos and Mexicans went unabated as they were often *indiscriminately* returned to Mexico. In all, the estimates of how many were sent back ranged from five hundred thousand to one million (Balderrama and Rodriguez, 1995; Acuna, 2007). High unemployment rates for Anglos and their increasing hysteria to deport Chicanos and Mexicans had been building since the late 1920s. Xenophobia, first extended toward Southern and Eastern European immigrants, was simply re-applied to Mexicans. Anglos were forced to take jobs they considered less than appropriate for themselves. Jobs they deemed beneath them suddenly became important enough to take. The loss of industrial jobs led many Anglo workers to seek employment in agricultural work. Unable to secure employment, and pressured to ease the high unemployment rates, Chicanos and Mexicans were given "transportation" to the border. Mexico being unable to provide employment for those who were sent back, Chicanos and Mexican immigrants simply moved back to the United States illegally.

The U.S. government felt it necessary to determine what to do about the *"Mexican Problem."* Despite the prior recruitment of Mexican laborers to fill labor shortages in mining, meatpacking, and sugar beet industries, the repatriation of Mexicans began. Some of the returnees went voluntarily, while others were forced. Government officials thought the best solution for Mexicans and Chicanos was their return to the motherland. At the time, Mexico was not economically stable enough to acquire some of the former countrymen. For many Chicanos, returning "illegally" to the United States was one way of moving back. Returning to the lives that had been disrupted was another thing to overcome. Families had been broken up and the financial costs to start over were difficult to overshadow their return.[4]

Adding to the furor toward Mexicans was the natural disaster occurring among Dust Bowl migrants. Prior to the Great Depression, the drought conditions which affected much of the Plains States and the South created unforeseen economic despair for Anglo workers. Unable to keep their jobs, entire families moved to states such as New Mexico and Texas. Others just kept going west and settled in California. The most popular destination was the Central Valley of California.

In short, this era of Mexican migration was a reminder that Mexican immigrants remained as temporary or second class citizens in America. Prior years of mistreatment toward Mexicans and Mexican Americans were recorded in the years 1821, 1848, and 1910. Each year marked the disrupted nature of the relationship between Mexicans, Mexican Americans, and Anglos. Rather than view the relationship improving, the next era only marked a different direction.

Bracero Era

The *Bracero Era* was a complete turn-around toward Mexico in terms of providing labor. Following a decade of restrictions and deportations, Mexican immigrants were again in demand as labor interests intensified with perceived labor shortages. Although the 1930s was an era known for deporting Chicano and Mexican immigrants, by 1939 there were signs of labor shortages. Labor shortages were increasingly being reported in agricultural work. Unable to find able-bodied American workers, agribusiness interests turned to the U.S. government for help. According to scholar Dr. Ernesto Garlarza, agribusiness was actively pursuing government help and was doing so with the loss of workers who were leaving the rural sectors and heading to urban employment. Indeed, Garlaza states:

> *These imbalances in the supply of labor and the demand of production were accentuated by the growth of war industry—shipbuilding, aircraft, steel, and oil refining. The new plants and shops in San Francisco, Vallejo, San Pedro, and San Diego drew thousands of migrants away from the Central Valley* (pg. 42).

Following the entrance of the United States into World War II, powerful agricultural business interests increased their search for temporary workers. The shortage of workers in agricultural sectors would result following the demand for war production workers. With the New Deal

---

[4] For an excellent account of this period of Chicano history, see Camille Guerin-Gonzalez's historical account, *Mexican Workers and the American Dreams: Immigration, Repatriation, and California Farm Labor, 1900-1939.*

policies of President Roosevelt in place, American workers were afforded the opportunity of industrial employment. Mexican Americans long denied industrial employment secured skilled jobs and also New Deal programs. Turning to the Fair Employment Practices Committee to fight against labor market discrimination, Mexican Americans gained access to high wage employment. *La Opinion* advertised defense industry jobs in Spanish, requiring no experience necessary, only a birth certificate required for employment. Not only were Mexican American men offered employment, but Mexican American women were also given the opportunity to work. Indeed, following in the footsteps of *Rosie the Riveter*, Mexican American women were offered jobs as riveters. Going from low paying jobs to skilled and higher paid jobs was monumental to Mexican Americans who were discriminated against from industrial employment prior to World War II. Rural to urban migration of workers ensued as industrial jobs in major cities were created to meet the demands of the production of tanks, military hardware, and manufactured goods. America was at war and workers were needed. Even young Chicanos acquired urban employment and, with their newly acquired income, engaged in wearing zoot-suits (Takaki, 2001).[5] Job growth was evident within the ship-building industry and steel industry.[6] In the midst of the increased need for industrial workers, agricultural labor interests took on a new emphasis toward labor recruitment.

The initial suggestion for a guest worker program was plausible given the economic and social ties the two countries had established. The Bracero Program existed for twenty-two years; this implies a great deal about the program's impact on U.S.-Mexico relations. The entrance of the United States into World War II further stimulated the recruitment of agricultural workers. One of the factors for the demand of labor was due to the apparent labor shortage. Workers who had been employed by agricultural work were beginning to find employment in the emerging military industrial labor force. Among them were Chicano workers. Rather than remain in unstable work, many Chicano workers were lured by higher wages and year round employment, leaving agricultural work behind Ranchers sought to relieve their labor shortages by proposing a guest worker program. Lobbied by intense agribusiness interests, U.S. government officials approached Mexico about the guest worker program. At first, Mexico was not completely thrilled with the thought of Mexican nationals going to the United States. The aftermath of the 1930s with the deportation of Mexicans and Mexican Americans as scapegoats for the high unemployment rate for Anglos was still fresh in the minds of Mexicans. The relationship between Mexico and the United States was strained due to the post effects of the repatriation movement.

Whether or not there was a labor shortage, agricultural interests persuaded the U.S. government to get the Mexican government to agree to a guest worker program. Previous guest worker programs were not new between Mexico and the United States. Recruitment of Mexican

---

[5] For an excellent analysis of the zoot-suit phenomenon see, Susan Marie Green, *Zoot Suiters: Past and Present.* (University of Minnesota, 1997, Ph.D. Thesis).

[6] Puerto Ricans were recruited to the mainland as part of the program called *Operation Famlift.* An account of the recruit of Puerto Ricans' experience was documented by Dennis Valdez. Valdez's book *Al Norte*, devotes an entire chapter.

immigrant workers during the first decades of the twentieth century served as a model despite not being labeled a guest worker program. Indeed, critics argue it was the *first* bracero program rather than the program of 1942 (Gomez-Quinones, 1994; Gonzalez, 2007).

The Bracero Program was organized and longer sustained than previous recruitment efforts. Indeed, after twenty-two years of its existence, Mexican workers signed over 4.6 million contracts taking advantage of working in the United States. On August 4, 1942, the agreement for a formal guest worker program between the United States and Mexico was signed under Public Law 45. The first braceros recruited were sent to Stockton, California, where they were greeted by a festive reception including a marching band and local politicians. This sort of reception was repeated for arriving braceros during the initial years of the program. A former bracero recalls his reception to the United States:

> *What caught my attention was that, and then which proved to be right, was that the first wave of braceros had a better experience. It was a wonderful experience. We came in first class trains, with rooms, and cafeterias .*

> (Interviewed in December 2001).

During its first year, over 4,000 braceros were contracted. As Table 1 indicates, the number of braceros contracted continually escalated and reached a peak in the 1950s. The program was

TABLE 1. *Mexican Braceros to the United States (1942-1964)*

Year	Braceros	Undocumented
1942	4,203	11,784
1943	52,098	11,175
1944	62,170	31,174
1945	49,454	69,164
1946	32,043	99,591
1947	19,632	193,657
1948	35,345	192,779
1949	107,000	288,253
1950	67,500	468,339
1951	192,000	509,040
1952	197,100	528,815
1953	201,380	885,587
1954	309,033	89,583
1955	398,650	254,096
1956	445,197	87,696
1957	436,049	59,918
1958	432,857	53,474
1959	437,643	45,336
1960	315,846	70,684
1961	291,420	88,823
1962	194,978	92,758
1963	186,865	88,712
1964	177,736	86,597
Total	**4,646,199**	**5,307,035**

Source: Corneluis, 1989

by all means a success for American agribusiness. Although designed to be a program for the duration of War World II, the program continually found support for its extension.

By 1947, enough pressure was asserted to extend the program until its demise in 1964. Despite its initial support for labor shortages, and with returning GIs, there continued a reason to import guest workers. The Bracero Program would go through a series of administrative branches which would direct its operation. It first began to operate through the INS (Immigration and Naturalization Service) and the Department of State, Justice, and Labor. The INS role was to ensure that Mexican braceros would follow a routine of regulated entries, departures, and complied with their temporary visas. On the Mexican side, the first program was the *Dirección General del Servicio Consular;* by the 1950s, the program was administered by the *Dirección de Asuntos de Trabajadores Agricolas Migratorios of the Secretaria de Relaciones Exteriores.* The agency on the Mexican side was to ensure the quotas of Mexican workers were met and were placed at the recruiting centers.

Although not initially intended, the railroad industry also participated in the recruitment of braceros. According to Barbara De Alvardo de Driscoll's (1999) study of Mexican bracero railroad workers, close to 47,000 were recruited over a six-year period. Beginning in 1943, the War Manpower Commission authorized braceros as workers for maintaining and constructing the railroads. Among the railroad industries employing braceros were the Southern Pacific; the Atchison, Topeka, Santa Fe; and Western Pacific. In 1949 the recruitment of bracero workers for the railroad industry was stopped.

One unintended consequence of the Bracero Program was the rise in the number of undocumented immigrants. By 1947 the Bracero Program had taken a different direction. No longer a wartime effort to recruit workers, the program was a peacetime activity and was viewed differently. The American public and public policy makers were focusing on the increased number of apprehensions of undocumented Mexican immigrants.

The Bracero Program unintentionally increased undocumented immigration, but immigrants from Mexico had migrated back and forth from Mexico long before the program was set in place. For Mexicans, the border could not separate families. Enticed by higher wages and family members living in the United States, undocumented immigration began to exceed the number of braceros contracted. Public demands for securing the border against undocumented immigrants from Mexico led to the development of *Operation Wetback.* The public support for the deportation of unwanted Mexicans intensified by the 1950s. Prior to the creation of *Operation Wetback,* the apprehensions of undocumented immigrants was getting little in the way of government support. Testimony from border officials from Texas by the late 1940s revealed that border agents were kept away from certain farms in South Texas (Garcia y Griego, 1996). Undocumented Mexican immigrant workers were valuable to Texas agricultural interests and governmental agencies were used to circumvent the law.

By the early 1950s, the anti-Mexican fever became too hot to control. In the minds of most Americans there were too many Mexicans entering the United States. This period also became known as the drying out of Mexican immigrants. Once at the border, Mexican immigrants who had been caught in the United States without papers were transported to the border and made to sign contracts to be let back in as braceros. An estimated 96,239 undocumented immigrants from Mexico were dried out during 1950 (Garcia and Griego, 1996). In that one year, more undocumented immigrants were legalized into the Bracero Program than braceros contracted in Mexico.

Despite the lax attitude toward undocumented immigrants, *Operation Wetback* succeeded in reducing the number of apprehensions. But it was short-lived. The rise in apprehensions began to increase again in the late 1950s. To counter the increased apprehensions, border agents would use a method called a "drying out" of wetbacks. Undocumented immigrants captured were turned into braceros. Once apprehended and returned to the border, they were directed to sign a bracero contract. The "drying out" program was said to have limited success in stopping the flow of undocumented immigration.

The *Bracero Era* was not without controversy. Due to the number of undocumented immigrants who continued to migrate to the United States, anti-Mexican attitudes continued despite the contributions of braceros. Texas was notorious for recruiting undocumented immigrants in response to being denied braceros at the beginning of the program. Texas was considered far to anti-Mexican with public displays of barring Mexicans from restaurants and hotels. By March 10, 1947, the state of Texas was certified access to braceros (Garcia and Griego, 1996). Although allowed to recruit braceros, the anti-Mexican feelings in Texas and other regions where braceros worked still continued.

Despite attempts to control the undocumented population of Mexican immigrants during the bracero era, Mexican immigrants continued to migrate north outside the program's control. Two factors seem to lay the groundwork for continued undocumented immigration: The first factor was that not all Mexicans were able to secure contracts. Either they were denied due to age, being too urban looking, or simply denied for not willing to pay bribes expected of potential recruits (Garlarza, 1964). The second factor was the intensity to find workers who would work for the lesser amount some growers insisted upon. Not wanting to pay the guaranteed wages mandated by the bracero contract, unscrupulous employers would simply supply themselves with undocumented Mexican immigrants.

Not until *Operation Wetback* were Mexican immigrants rounded up and taken to the border if they were found to be in the country without papers.. Starting on June 17, 1954, military run operations occurred in Southern California to round up undocumented Mexican immigrants. The program was to be extended to the Midwest, Pacific Northwest, and Texas. Considered a success by some, the number of undocumented immigrants did remain far below the previous years. However, it's hard not to discount how many undocumented Mexican immigrants may have been rounded up and legalized at the border. In short, the effects of *Operation Wetback* may have been the increased number of Mexican immigrants who were not counted as undocumented immigrants.

The final years of the Bracero Program would be met by increased domestic resistance to the program. Scholar-activist Dr. Ernesto Garlarza led a public cry for the Bracero Program to be dismantled. Arguing that braceros left little opportunity for domestic organizing of laborers in agriculture, Dr. Garlarza wrote about the program's harmful affects to wages, its undermining of strikes, and its creation of horrible working conditions. With the publishing of his book, *Merchants of Labor: The Mexican Bracero Story*, Garlarza (1964) was able to document the abuses of the Bracero Program.

On the Mexican side, the Mexican government was reluctant to see the program end. There was concern with the program ending that it would have an adverse economic effect upon the Mexican economy. With braceros set to return, there was concern that the Mexican economy would be unable to absorb the extra workers. Former braceros returned to Mexico only for a short time, and then they began to return to the United States beginning in the late 1960s. The years of bracero migration set the path for further documented and undocumented immigration. Mexican immigration would continue well into the next two decades.

Undocumented Era

The *Undocumented Era* followed the end of the Bracero Program. The post effects of twenty-two years of stimulated migration led to increased migration rather than decreased migration (Massey and Liang, 1989; Cerrutti and Massey, 2004). Numerous studies on the continued migration of Mexican immigrants after the end of the Bracero Program suggested that the social networks created from the program ensured a sustained flow of migrants (Warren and Passel, 1987; Passel and Woodrow, 1987). In addition, economic issues on both sides of the border throughout the decades added to the net flow. An examination of the number of Mexican immigrants who entered the United States during the years following the end of the program confirmed that Mexican migration created an annual influx of migrants across the border. Indeed, 386,000 permanent resident visas were issued to Mexicans from 1960 to 1968. The increased reliance on Mexican immigrant labor in the agricultural sector in the United States further guaranteed that immigration from Mexico continued.

Throughout the 1960s and 1970s, the migration came from largely traditional areas of Mexico. According to most studies, the states of Jalisco, Michoacan, and Guanajuato sent the majority of Mexican immigrants following the end of the Bracero Program. In addition, immigration in the late 1960s and 1970s was a mixture of documented and undocumented immigration (Durand, Massey, and Charvert, 2000). The documented immigrants were made up of former braceros and family members seeking to settle in the United States.

A surge in population growth along the border following the demise of the Bracero Program created a new problem for the Mexican government. The interior migration of Mexicans toward the border looking for employment created a surplus of labor. Industrialization of the border region took on new dimensions. In 1965, the authorization of the Border Industrialization Program (BIP) helped to generate employment. BIP offered Mexican workers improved skills and increased personal income (Tiano, 1985). The industrialization effort along the border region became known popularly as the Maquiladora Program. Through binational concessions, U.S. corporations set up their operations along the border region to produce products that would be exported to the United States. Ex-braceros were thought to be the ones likely to work at the border region factories. As it turned out, young female Mexican workers were hired instead (Tiano, 1994). The Maquiladora Program has not accomplished what it was intended to do.

During the late 1960s and 1970s, the idea of re-creating another bracero-like program was discussed. President Echeverria had to be talked out of such a plan by Ernesto Garlarza. In his State of the Union Address in 1976, President Echeverria pointed out his opposition to another temporary guest worker program. President Echeverria found that guest worker programs did not deter undocumented immigration.

By the 1970s, the rise in the number of undocumented immigrants from Mexico was again creating public policy concerns. In Texas, legislation to limit education to Mexican immigrant children created a division. On the one hand, employers continued to need Mexican immigrant workers. But others in Texas objected to undocumented immigrant children receiving free access to public funded education (Flores, 1984).

Indeed, by the late 1970s, undocumented Mexican immigration came back on the national radar after a brief decline. One suggestion for the brief decline of undocumented immigration from Mexico was the provisions passed in the *1965 Immigration Act*. The passage of the *1965 Immigration Act* allowed increased quotas for Western Hemisphere immigrants, particularly from Mexico. Mexican immigrants could legalize their residency through the kinship provision.

With the election of President Ronald Reagan, a new policy on immigration from Mexico was discussed. One method for dealing with undocumented immigration from Mexico was a "voluntary departure order." In short, undocumented immigrants left the United States without a court hearing and would cross back over as quickly as possible. By the 1980s, the Border Patrol and the undocumented immigrants were playing what scholars categorized as a game of "cat and mouse" (Chavez, 1994; Koussoundji, 1992).

The Reagan Administration sought to ease the tension among its conservative supporters by legislation to ease the flow. One solution proposed was to allow undocumented immigrants the opportunity to legalize their status. The legalization of undocumented immigrants was at the top of the Reagan agenda. In 1986, Reagan signed into law the *Immigration and Reform Control Act*. IRCA would allow undocumented immigrants to file for permanent legal status if they could prove they had been in the United States prior to January 1, 1982. The number of Mexican immigrants who took advantage of the one-time offer was estimated at 2.3 million. One of the changes resulting from the new law was the flow of Mexican immigrants changed from being seasonal migrants to permanent settlers. Indeed, the number of apprehensions following the law's enactment fell from 1.6 million in 1986 to 830,000 by 1989.

Post-IRCA Era

The final era of immigration has been labeled the *Post-IRCA*. Despite attempts to stem the flow of immigrants from Mexico, studies revealed significant shifts in the migration pattern. Cornelius found evidence that Mexicans were coming from different regions of Mexico. Rather than coming from traditional central regions such as Jalisco and Michoacan, they were coming from the North and South. Immigrants arrived from areas such as Baja California, Chihuahua, Oaxaca, and Guerrero. Also, the characteristics of Mexican migrants during the 1980s shifted from the rural male migrant to the urban educated migrant

(Corneluis, 1993). The conditions for the migration for women to enter the migration pattern also occurred (Hondagneu-Sotelo, 2007; Donato and Patterson, 2006). Service sector employment of Latina domestic workers in the city of Los Angeles helped stimulate the migration of Mexican and Central American women. Indeed, Sociologists Hondagneu-Sotelo argues that rather than see a decrease in the demand for domestic workers, Latina immigrant workers found increasing employment in the expanding service sector. In short, no longer was migration from Mexico and Central America a male phenomenon. Women migrants had now joined the migration pattern as the global economy further tied the U.S. economy to developing Latin American economies.

The 1990s did not experience a decline in the number of undocumented immigrants; rather, conditions in Mexico and the United States continued to ensure the demand for Mexican immigrants. Indeed, the post-IRCA effects led to increased migration of undocumented Mexican immigration. The increase of undocumented immigration was not expected after IRCA was passed according to Durand, Massey, and Parrado:

> *As an enforcement policy intended to control undocumented migration, however, IRCA was an unequivocal failure. Not only did it fail to deter undocumented migrants from leaving Mexico, but it actually encouraged additional undocumented migration by family and friends who had remained behind and it was instrumental in transforming a predominately rural, male, and temporary flow of migrant workers into a feminized, urbanized, and permanent population of settled immigrants (1999).*

Under the Clinton Administration, attempts at a hard line position toward undocumented immigration were seen. On various occasions in the 1990s, public support of government intervention toward controlling undocumented immigration from Mexico occurred. In California, undocumented immigrants were the target for restrictions as Proposition 187 passed on November 1995. The continued wave of undocumented immigrants from Mexico concerned the Clinton Administration. With names such as *Operation Hold the Line, Operation Gatekeeper*, and *Operation Safeguard* various border enforcement programs were enacted to secure the border (Nevin, 2002). Although there were temporary drops in the apprehension of undocumented immigrants along the border, the real truth of the matter was the redirecting of immigrants to more remote areas to cross. By the mid 1990s, the number of deaths along the border increased. In an attempt to decrease the number of deaths along the border, churches organized relief groups to set up jugs of water marked by blue flags at popular crossing points. The tension between Mexico and the United States only increased due to the Mexican government's intervention to protect Mexican immigrants crossing the border at unprecedented rates. The Mexican government began issuing satellite tracking devices. An estimated 200,000 devices were said to be given out in 2008. Estimates that six million undocumented immigrants from Mexico are currently living and working in the United States has called for tougher enforcement of security.

Other measures have been proposed in terms of a comprehensive immigration policy that would lead to the path of citizenship. At this point, nothing has been secured by either side of the debate regarding Mexican immigration. One thing is for certain, increased militarization of the border has led to the mixed results. Indeed, as the border becomes difficult to maneuver, Mexican immigrants are less likely to migrate back and forth. Mexican migrants tend to remain in the United States rather than take the chance of apprehension.

More recent analysis on the current migration of Mexicans to the United States has focused on new settlement patterns. One recent publication found that Mexican immigrants are heading toward non-traditional migration areas. The Southwest and Midwest have had a longer period of Mexican immigrant *enganches*. But since the 1990s, the pattern has changed. Robert Smith's book, *Mexican New York: Transnational Lives of New Immigrants*, examines the migration of Ticaunense community members. Americans are witnessing increased Mexican migration to the East Coast and the South. These non-traditional settlement regions create new questions for immigrant scholars regarding settlement and population growth. In the early 1990s, the mere mention of Mexicans migrating to the East Coast or the South was not on most scholars' radar. The migration experience of Latinos to those regions prior to the 1990s was of Puerto Ricans, Dominicans, Cubans, and other Central and Latin American immigrants (Portes and Bach, 1985; Grasmuck and Pessar, 1991; Levitt, 2001).

Finally, a recent analysis of Mexican immigration is the book, *New Destinations: Mexican Immigration in the United States* by Víctor Zúñiga and Rubén Hernández-León. Published in 2006, the editors of the book offer readers multiple views of Mexican migration to the United States. The book's authors focus on different regions of new settlement for Mexican immigrants. In short, the book offers insights into what is expected from future migration. Mexican immigration to the United States is no longer situated to one region; multiple regions are now the latest destinations of Mexican immigrants. Recruitment to work in meatpacking factories or the Kentucky racehorse industry is becoming more common today. With Mexico bursting at the seams with its growing population, a new set of potential migrants emerges. If Mexico's economy continues to underachieve, migration will continue. Mexicans will opt to migrate north as many others have done throughout the twentieth century.

Conclusion

Today the demand for cheap labor within the agricultural sector is even more immediate. Fearing the inability to compete with other foreign producers of fresh vegetables, American farmers are seeking to cut costs. One method for competing with foreign farmers is having access to temporary workers. Mexican immigrants continue to fill the needs of American farmers. Other sectors of the U.S. economy are also seeking labor which is cheap and accessible. As more American workers have moved away from jobs considered less desirable, researchers are finding a growing number of Mexican and other immigrant workers working in such industries as meat packing (Grey and Woodrick, 2002).

However, the growing anti-immigrant group movement is determined to slow the number of undocumented immigrants who enter the country each year. There are two opposing sides: Those who wish to continue to have access to cheap temporary labor and those who seek to limit the amount of undocumented immigrants. Caught in the middle of this dynamic are the Mexican immigrants who continue to migrate despite the barriers placed in front of them.

The United States wants its labor supply supplemented by Mexican immigrants. The American public wants, in general, to see that the border is secured. Border security is especially on the minds of most Americans during this post-9/11 era. Both do not seem possible without a compromise of sorts. Another guest worker program would only continue what has been the legacy of Mexican immigration, recruitment, and settlement.

CHAPTER 2

Braceros and Recruitment

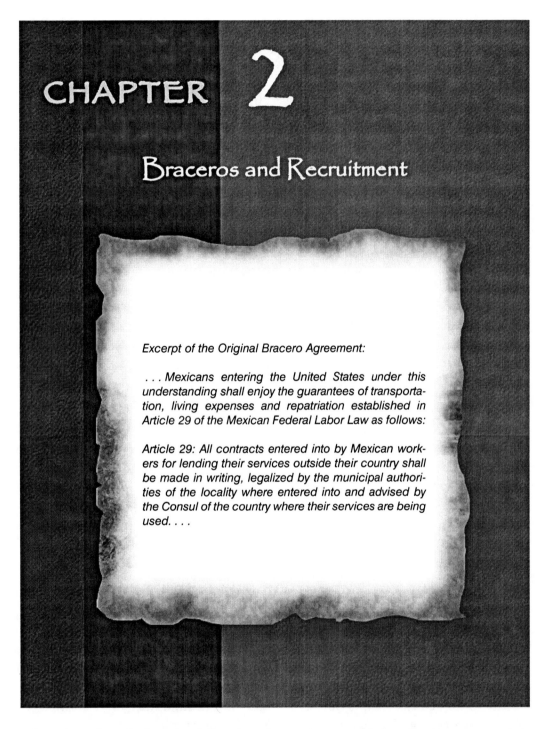

Excerpt of the Original Bracero Agreement:

. . . Mexicans entering the United States under this understanding shall enjoy the guarantees of transportation, living expenses and repatriation established in Article 29 of the Mexican Federal Labor Law as follows:

Article 29: All contracts entered into by Mexican workers for lending their services outside their country shall be made in writing, legalized by the municipal authorities of the locality where entered into and advised by the Consul of the country where their services are being used. . . .

One of my best friends from childhood and I made an unlikely pair. He was much bigger than I; by the time we reached eighth grade, he was close to 210 pounds and I was a mere 80 pounds…if that. In my eight years at Our Lady of Guadalupe School, I was always the smallest among the boys. My friend was always the biggest kid in my eight-year tenure. One benefit of our friendship was that I could avoid potential fights with other kids. I recall that by ninth grade he was already shaving. It would take me until my early twenties before I had to shave every day. I used to catch a ride on his ten-speed bike on the way home from school.

I would sit on the bicycle rack and hold on until we made our way through the city streets. The rack gave me no comfort on the bumps along the way. I knew where the hardest bumps were, and tried to anticipate them; but it was rare to miss the steel burning into my small unpadded cheeks. The worst bumps were the curbs when there were no driveways to use. My friend would go on to high school and junior college and become a football star at both levels. Even though by conventional football standards he was not overly tall, he was extremely agile for someone his size. For reasons I still can't quite figure out, he turned down an offer to attend Dartmouth College to play football.

We hung out together since we only lived a few blocks away from each other. I recall when he was in third or fourth grade he would go home to help his father build the home my friend still lives in today. His father was reluctant for me to stay and visit because he wanted his son to change his clothes and get to his chores. So I would say goodbye and walk the rest of the way home. I don't know the complete story, but according to my best friend, his father had come to the United States as a Mexican bracero. He worked on the railroads and later became a resident of the United States. My friend had lost his mother when he was in first grade so it was only the two of them. His father did remarry at one point but the marriage was more of convenience rather than mutual love. I did meet the second wife and I really didn't feel it was a comfortable marriage, even though I was still a grammar school kid at the time. His father divorced his second wife and never married again, but he did have a long-time girlfriend until his untimely death.

Had I known I would be writing this book on the former Bracero Program many years later, I would have certainly used the opportunity to document his father's story. What I can tell you about my former college roommate and long time friend is that he is a multi-millionaire today. His father began to buy property and rebuild homes to rent back to the same people who lived there. Over the years my friend's father bought many properties—I lost count. In one block area only, there are six new rebuilt homes. This is one of the success stories of a former bracero with the entrepreneur spirit. It is this type of story that illuminates the long-term effects of guest worker programs.

As critics of guest worker programs have argued, there is nothing more permanent than temporary guest workers (Martin, 2001; Briggs, 2004). Scholar Philip Martin suggests that guest worker programs help to increase documented and undocumented immigration. Martin argues that distortion and dependence are factors for documented and undocumented immigration resulting from guest worker programs. Distortion refers to the flexibility of labor markets and economies and their adjustments to the absence or presence of foreign workers. Dependence is the reliance of individuals, families, and communities on the earnings from foreign workers working abroad. In the end, recruitment of guest workers, whether to the United States or other countries, leads to further migration and settlement (Casltes, 1986).

Although the concept of guest worker programs are proposed as a solution for relieving labor shortages, the recruitment of immigrant workers creates other potential consequences. Indeed, contract agreements allowing temporary workers should address the long-term effects of settlement. Mexico and the United States labor recruitment efforts offer insight into the process of guest worker programs. Since 1848, Mexico and the United States have shared a border that continues to be constantly redefined. There will be no time, now or in the future, when the border between the two countries will not determine public policy. Recruitment of Mexican immigrants continues that legacy. Recruitment leads to further permanent social ties between the two countries. Today, Mexican immigrants have new sources that maintain their ties to the United States. Indeed, there is no shortage of cell phones, computers, and other forms of technology that can deter Mexican immigrants from being informed and connected to their families back in Mexico. If current technological trends continue, the 2000 mile border between Mexico and the United States will eventually be a rusting, hole-ridden, graffiti covered, and seldom maintained fence. The physical fence along the border will be an "aging" deterrent to further migration.

Frequently the legacy of the former U.S-Mexico Bracero Program is only discussed as a historical antiquated footnote to the current debate on immigration reform. A recent news article on the proposed settlement paying the 10 percent savings owed to the braceros who entered the program from 1942-1946[1] once again reminded the nation of yet another post-effect of the program's legacy. Reported in the *Los Angeles Times* (Bloomekatz, 2008),[2] "*Ex-Braceros get 2 Months to File Claims for up to $3,500*," the article addressed the lawsuit settlement to pay former braceros:

> *The United States relied on Mexican laborers to bolster its workforce during World War II, but activists and lawyers claimed for years that many of those workers were never fully compensated. More than six decades later and after a lengthy court battle, thousands of the bracero guest workers may finally get a chance to collect their full pay.*

Of course this examination allows for a further analysis of the relationship years after the "dirty" deed of recruitment has occurred. Chicano families can trace their family history to the Bracero Program. As pointed out in the introduction, some of the oral histories I've collected are from personal contacts I met through my students and colleagues. The U.S.-Mexico border for Chicanos is more about saving enough money to pay a smuggler or coyote to help them cross (Donato, Wagner, and Patterson, 2008). The social ties that bound us all to families, friends, and employers makes the border for Chicanos merely a barrier constructed to imply restrictions to keep "unwanted" groups out. By contrast, the border is seen by non-Chicanos as being enforceable, deterring those whom they believe harmful to their way of life. Recruitment of Mexican immigrants only strengthens increased settlement and strict draconian measures are less likely to ease migration over the long run. Indeed, attempts at strict border enforcement encourage migrants not to risk apprehension returning home (Wilson, 1999).

---

[1] According to several news reports the wage settlement was extended to include all former braceros who came during the twenty-two year history of program. Initially the settlement was excluded to the braceros who came during the 1942-1946 period of the program when the 10 percent wage deductions occurred.

[2] Two days later, the period for filling out the required information for the lost wages was given an additional month. An error in the claim form was the reason for the extended period.

This chapter examines the recruitment process of former braceros, which begins as a short-term proposal but ends in long-term consequences. Previous examinations of recruitment of braceros exist, but they lack the substance of first-hand accounts. Only a small number of recent studies have employed oral histories to examine the recruitment process of braceros (Gonzalez, 2007; Mize, 2006; Rosas, 2006). This chapter will add to the public discourse of guest worker recruitment. Employing the oral histories of former braceros, the chapter will rely upon first-hand accounts of their experiences. Following the social capital theory line of reasoning, recruitment begins the process of initial migration. However, over time, migrants use their first migration experience to make additional trips. Building upon their social capital, migrants are therefore able to lower the cost of migration and increase their net returns.

The analysis will have the foresight that former braceros are no longer migrating. Now reaching their *golden years*, former braceros are less a part of the current migration stream. Indeed, braceros are past the age when migrating is to financially support their families. Most former braceros are at the age which begins to limit their movement between the two countries. In previous examinations, braceros were still relatively young and were not considered done migrating (Massey and Liang, 1989). In addition, recent examinations did not account for the age of braceros who are now elderly (Garcia and Garcia, 2005; Schmitter-Heisler, 2007). Indeed, a recent *New York Times* article (Porter and Malkins, 2005) pointed out that the growing elderly population of Mexican immigrants in the United States is a public policy concern:

> *What will happen when the 10 million Mexicans living in the United States become too old to work?*

Officials and analysts on both sides of the border not only focus their attention on the continued inflow of illegal workers, but also they have many concerns about the future of these aging immigrants.

What began as a means to temporarily fill the labor shortages in sectors of the U.S. economy largely became a permanent recruitment of temporary workers. Now, forty to sixty years removed from the program's initial implementation, former braceros are in the United States permanently or have returned to Mexico to live out their elderly years. Today these former guest workers have families and their children are reaching middle age themselves. Some of the children of braceros were born in Mexico, while others were born in the United States and are second generation Mexican Americans (Ortiz and Telles, 2008: Bautista-Hayes, 2004). Indeed, the topic of the former Bracero Program remains relative to current immigration policy. My examination of the former braceros now more than forty years (or longer) removed from their initial migration provides a unique opportunity to examine their initial recruitment.

Braceros Today

As of this writing, these former braceros are less likely to be migrating back and forth. Visits to Mexico are more likely to check on personal property (i.e., homes) or to remain in contact with extended family members. During their primary working years, former braceros were migrating back and forth. Former braceros today, whose age can range from their sixties through their nineties, reflects a different period in their lives. They have reached an age at which they are more likely to be less active within the labor market, thus giving researchers the opportunity to examine their permanent status as settled immigrants. The former braceros (2.6 million who signed contracts to work in the United States) are the permanent legacy of guest workers. Their legacy endures as permanent fixtures with families and their children. In short, this analysis attempts to fill the gap between the prior (i.e., historical) examinations of the former U.S-Mexico Bracero Program and the current age of former braceros, as the stories of these elderly former guest workers need to be documented. An interview with an elderly bracero, Don Benjamin Munoz, revealed his state of mind regarding his immediate future:

> **Paul:** Did you ever think that you would stay in the country for so long?
>
> **Don Benjamin:** No, I never thought it would happen. I took care of my children's legal status with the thought that they would continue their education in Mexico. However, they all continued with their education here; most finished high school and a few went to one or two years of college. After a while, most started working and soon married. My whole family is here now. I don't see any reason for me going back to Mexico.
>
> (Interview with Benjamin Munoz 2003)

Previous studies of Mexican immigrants in the United States have been conducted. Mario Gamio's account of Mexican immigrants during the period known as the *Engagche* period remains a remarkable historical account to this day. Published in 1971, a forty-year period from its initial publication in 1931, the stories are remarkable for their original accounts of the experiences of Mexican immigrants. I attempt to capture that same originality given the amount of time that has passed since the program's ending in 1964. Sixty to forty plus years since their initial migration, the stories of former braceros need to be preserved for future generations of scholars.

One study which examined the settlement of former braceros by Massey and Liang (1989) was conducted while they were still migrating from Mexico. What makes this prior study important to cite is the relative age of the former braceros at the time of the publication. According to the demographic background information from the Massey and Liang study, the average age of the former braceros was fifty-six years. A current estimate of the age of those braceros as of this writing (2009) would be eighty-two years. At fifty-six years of age, most of those former braceros were likely still engaging in work and migrating. By their current average ages, most would be in their retirement years. The authors argued that former braceros were likely to be migrating long after their bracero contracts had ended. Indeed, they suggested the following theoretical line of reasoning:

> *Migration is inherently dynamic and social, so that guest workers do not just stop migrating when their visas expire, and immigration does not cease when labor recruitment ends. Rather, the act of migration itself changes guest worker's aspirations, desires, and motivations, as well as the perceived costs and returns of movements, and leads to more migration.*
>
> (Massey and Liang, 1989)

In short, recruitment is only the first step in what turns out to be a long-term phenomenon. What appears to be a short-term solution to labor shortages with the agreement of guest worker programs becomes inherently a long-term permanent settlement. Notwithstanding another guest worker program, the United States is less likely to ensure another generation of migration from Mexico similar to the long-term effects of the former U.S.-Mexico Bracero Program.

Recruitment as a Social Capital

Sociological research has argued that immigrant labor recruitment is a social process. Enticing a reserve supply of workers willing to migrate abroad is essential by potential employers (Massey, Durand and Malone, 2002; Portes and Bach, 1985; Portes and Rubaut, 2006). The history of recruitment of immigrant workers to the United States indicates that recruiters must devise ways to lure potential workers (Takaki, 1989; Daniels, 2002). Avenues toward tapping into a pool of potential recruits include recruitment ads and recruiters. As indicated in Chapter One, Mexican immigrants were recruited throughout the twentieth century. In some cases, the recruitment of Mexican immigrants was aggressive and forceful. Once recruited, both sending and receiving countries begin a relationship that continues beyond the initial stages of recruitment and return migration. In many prior cases, potential immigrants were expected to come temporarily. Recruitment was expected to be a temporary solution to labor shortages.

The recruitment of braceros employed similar recruitment methods, such as government ads, and radio and newspaper announcements in Mexico (Galarza, 1964). Previously (Chapter One), I discussed how Mexican immigrants were recruited to the United States as temporary workers. However, many former immigrant workers from Mexico have stayed in the United States following their initial experience. Similar stories can be found among many former immigrant workers who recruited to work in the United States. However, those who decided to stay often did so at a cost.

Due to the ill effects of the deportation of Mexicans and Mexican Americans in the 1930s, the United States was hard pressed to prove that it was not discriminating against Mexican workers. According to Balderama and Rodriguez's study (1996) of the reparation movement, they found that many Mexican and Mexican Americans were still reeling from the reparations of the 1930s; indeed, the Mexican government was not at ease about allowing Mexicans to once again migrate to the United States.

The history and legacy of the reparations of former Mexican nationals had remained among the Mexican populace. Don Cipriano Santillan speaks of his knowledge about how he became informed about the program:

> *When the government announced that they would be giving this opportunity with the bracero program, the entire country found out. So people came from all different areas. People would find out where and find a means of getting there. Not everyone went to the same place. It would get very dark, it happened to some of us, it happened to me. Since it got dark, people would line up. The sun would rise and people would be standing there. Until they started reading off the list and that's*

when you would go to where the job required you to go. You had to wait to see if they would call your name. Sometimes three or four days, even a week to see if they would call you. And that's how it went, but also in the citadel, there was lots of suffering. In the middle of the night there was lots of people standing out in the cold.

(Interview with Cipriano Santillan 2004)

Many braceros found out about the program through word of mouth. But recruitment was still the most important means of getting potential Mexican workers to enter the program. Once the knowledge of the program was available, Mexicans were responsible for finding the nearest recruitment center. The different accounts offer interesting insights toward how potential braceros made their decisions to come to the United States through the program. In the account below, this former bracero had plans to be a professional soccer player. He also did not have the background of a field hand; rather, he had been an urban city dweller. Recruiters were only interested in obtaining those who had prior farm experience. Here is the account of how he made it to the contractors in Mexico City:

My friend and I did not plan on coming to the U.S. We did not have the education to do so. While I played soccer in Mexico along with a friend, our mentality focused on playing and getting recruited by a team rather than coming to the United States. But when we went to Mexico City, my brother-in-law, who married my sister, had an apartment in Mexico City and we asked him if we could spend the night over. He also had apartments in Laredo and other places. When we got to Mexico City we went to see if he could lend us the apartment. He was kind and gave us the keys. My friend, who at the time was married, was telling me that he was making $12.50 a day in the US. This was in 1952. He asked me if I wanted to go with him, and in trying to convince me he also told me that he was very close to the Minister of Interior Relations Don Francisco De La Rocha. Basically he was telling me that he had a way to get me to the United States. I told him that I had never worked in my life and it was not going to happen. He kept trying to convince me and my friend by telling us how much he made and he went on. Finally, we went dressed up to see the Minister, and my brother-in-law introduced both of us to the Minister. I changed my mind and decided to come as well as my friend. We spoke to the Minister again to make sure that we wanted to go and he gave us a letter. That letter went through the President of Mexico. It was a very powerful letter. We came; we traveled and got in with the letter even though we faced minimal problems when crossing. Both of us had not been really dismissed from the army so a general came with us. We were about to be sent back but the general showed them the letter and told immigration that the Minister had recommended us.

(Interview with Amado Carrasco 2002)

As information regarding the Bracero Program reached into other areas of Mexico, it wasn't long before each recruiting center was overwhelmed with potential recruits. As the example above suggests, friends or family members who had gone through the program or who had been to the United States would encourage others to join the program. Word of mouth was an important recruiting mechanism for supplying potential applicants for the program. Sociologists have documented this phenomenon regarding the process of social capital that builds from the experience of migrants. Social capital refers to the mechanism which becomes in place when migrants are able to provide shelter, job information, and fewer risks for other migrants to migrate abroad (Coleman, 1988; Massey and Liang, 1989). Indeed, other migrants are able to migrate more easily through the networks of family and friends who help facilitate the costs of migrating. As the news of the Bracero Program spread to remote areas of Mexico, poor Mexicans from rural areas emerged to attempt to enroll in the program.

As prior research has concluded, guest worker programs tend to offer potential migrants the opportunity to migrate and then continue to migrate after their contracts are completed. In Massey and Liangs's examination of the former U.S.-Mexico Bracero Program's post effect on immigration, they argued that. . . "Guest worker programs provide a reliable and stable institutional framework within which social ties can be formed between migrants and employers and between the migrants themselves." As their study concluded, the former Bracero Program created, and later maintained, social ties that made future migration possible.

Recruiting Settlers

The documentation of recruitment of Mexican immigrants to the United States has been examined by historians (Driscoll, 1999; Sanchez, 1995; Gomez-Quinones, 1994). The countless number of studies of Mexican migration to the United States often depicts migrants in the aggregate, which does not account for the personal stories of many Mexican immigrants who often had to make tremendous sacrifices to come from Mexico to the United States (Massey and Liang, 1989; Reichert and Massey, 1980). The examination of the recruitment of braceros would put a human face to the discourse of migration and guest worker programs. Indeed, many years have passed since the braceros I interviewed for the book first came to the United States. But their stories remain relative to the current discourse on proposed guest worker discussions. As recent as 2007, President Bush mentioned in his State of the Union speech, a proposal for a guest worker program:

> . . . we cannot fully secure the border unless we take pressure off the border—and that requires a temporary worker program. We should establish a legal and orderly path for foreign workers to enter our country to work on a temporary basis. As a result, they won't have to try to sneak in, and that will leave Border Agents free to chase down drug smugglers and criminals and terrorists. We'll enforce our immigration laws at the work site and give employers the tools to verify the legal status of their workers, so there's no excuse left for violating the law.
>
> (President Bush, State of the Union Speech, January 2007)

According to the social capital theory argument, immigrants begin to change their behavior according to their increased knowledge of recruiting countries. Unlike the neo-liberal argument which suggests that migrants simply decide to immigrate on the cost-benefits rational, the social capital theory suggests that initial migration trips can turn into several trips as migrants increase their knowledge of the host country. Social networks begin to lower the cost, and migration is further enhanced. For the braceros I interviewed, migration to the United States was already a part of their families' history. Don Salvador Munoz revealed his work experience in the United States before contracting as a bracero:

> **Paul:** Prior to coming as a bracero, did you ever come to work here in the United States?
>
> **Don Salvador:** Yes I worked in Buena Park picking strawberries.

Additionally, Don Salvador Munoz told me that members of his community had prior migration experience before coming as braceros. So the view of the program was already potentially in his thoughts:

> **Paul:** How did you find out about the Bracero Program?
>
> **Don Salvador:** Well, the thought of coming to work in the U.S. was always in my mind, even since I was a kid. Right after completing my military service, I decided to come. There must have been at least 150 men in my town that completed their service in 1959, and out of those 150, not one stayed in Mexico. All of us came, and the wave of immigrants took place every year. The following took place in my days: First, everyone had to commit one year of military service and then most ended up coming to the U.S. Things have changed now; most males come even before they reach 18 years of age. In my days you had to show proof of military service before coming to the U.S. Prior to my coming, a lot of my family members and neighbors had come to the U.S. to work. Coming to the U.S. was something expected out of everyone in my town.
>
> **Paul:** Did you ever ask them about their experience as braceros?
>
> **Don Salvador:** Well everyone knew how long the contracts were. I knew about a contract in Santa Paula that lasted 18 years. I'm not sure whether the contract lasted the 18 years or if the contract was occasionally renewed. Those working under this contract got the most out of it.

Prior migration and knowledge of the United States was evident by other relatives who had migrated north. One former bracero who I met through a friend of my brother-in-law came from the urban area and would eventually become successful as a musician. Don Reynaldo Aceves recalls hearing about the program from one of his uncle's relatives:

> **Paul:** Did you know other people that had been in the program and did you know where they were working?
>
> **Don Reynaldo:** Yes, I believe it was one of my uncle's relatives. He was here for about six months, and from what I heard he made lots of money. He worked overtime and dressed in fancy clothes every time he came. This only inspired me to come the following year.

Below Don Francisco Llamas talked about his recruitment through his family's prior knowledge of the United States:

Paul: How did you find out about this program? Was it because of your brother migrating?

Don Francisco: Yes, because he came first and I wanted to come as well after him.

Paul: Were you excited to know about the program? Did you think that your brother's experience was positive?

Don Francisco: Yes. I wanted to come here as well. I think my brother was like my dad because when my dad came he wanted to too. And when my dad came and went back, when he got there my brother was very happy he returned.

Paul: How old were you when you first came?

Don Francisco: I had just turned twenty.

Without some family history of migration, braceros heard about the program from information circulated by the popular media in Mexico. Don Agustin Alamanza, who is now living his elder years in a modest home in Santa Barbara, California, learned of the program through newspaper information. Physically disabled, but cared for by his daughters and grandchildren, he spoke on how he learned about the program:

> Yes, we knew where to go. We found out about it through the newspaper. At that time, hiring was taking place at the National Stadium in Mexico City. As soon as we got there, we took a taxi to the stadium. Once at the stadium, we were told to come the next day early in the morning. We had to be there at eight o'clock in the morning; however, we were there at seven o'clock. As soon as the doors opened, we were two of the firsts to fill out the contract.
>
> (Interview with Agustin Alamanza 2002)

The first braceros recall how they were treated by local communities. Indeed, the early participating braceros experienced local celebrations welcoming their contributions. Being among some of the first braceros to the United States, Don Ramon Martinez recalls being greeted with bands and local celebrations. Don Martinez recalls the confusion of local government officials as they had expected peasants from Mexico to be the first wave of braceros. Instead, the first braceros were not farm workers, but city dwellers who took the opportunity to work in the United States. Whether city dwellers or from the rural areas, many Mexican males were recruited into the Bracero Program and they sought to reap the benefits of international migration. Don Ramon Martinez describes his welcome to California:

> . . . We rode all night and arrived the next day in Sacramento around 3 PM. In Sacramento a group of women was waiting for us playing different types of music. The government was confused because it expected poor farm workers in sandals when instead what it got was a wave of city people.
>
> (Interview with Ramon Martinez 2003)

Recruiters from the United States were looking for workers who had field experience. However, the first bracero recruits were from urban areas. Some would use the program to find other careers in the United States. Recruiters were fooled by urban Mexicans who used various deceptive methods to get around inspections to see if they had prior farming experience. Passing the inspections of those who would choose the select few would make potential braceros dress down in order to "fool" the inspectors, as suggested by this former bracero's account:

> *The majority of the people did often scratch their hands with rocks or dirt in order to make them dirty and rough. Some even dressed in their worst clothes, trying to pass for poor and hard working peasants.*
>
> (Interview with Benjamin Munoz 2003)

The stories illustrate the problems associated with the recruitment process and the difficulties most of the braceros experienced at the hands of government officials and others involved with the program's implementation. Indeed, the description of the recruitment process provided by the participants suggested numerous problems for potential recruits. As I interviewed former braceros, I wanted to know why they decided to join the program. One former bracero described his decision based on his family's responsibilities:

> *In those times, I was training for the military service. I used to train every weekend as part of the service program. I was planning on working for the service, however, the pay was not enough to support my family. When I found out about the program, I decided to apply. A lot of people would discourage others by telling them that if they came they would be enlisted in the war. But I had to give it a shot.*
>
> (Interview with Alejandro Gomez 2002)

It is all too easy to see migration as an economic activity due to the wage differences between Mexico and the United States. Some decisions were made by families who had to let their sons join the program not sure what the economic outcome would be. A former barcero recalls why he decided to join the program:

> (Yes) . . . when I went to Texas I got a contract in Aguascalientes. My dad met the governor of Zacatecas. My dad helped him. The governor told him that if one day he needed something to go to Zacatecas. One night, I went out and I saw groups of people were loaded onto trucks in town. I questioned what they were going to do with all the people and they told me that they were contracted to go and work in the United States. The next day I went to visit my dad and I told him what happened. I told him that I wanted to go to the U.S. He told me that he did not have any money to send me there, so I told him that we needed to find a way. We had two bulls and a cow. We lost a cow in the mountain range and he told me to go and look for it and to forget about going. I found the cow and I wanted to have breakfast. My parents were not at the house, only my younger brothers. My brothers and I cleaned the maize field. They told me that my parents had gone to the town, so I left without having breakfast. I found my parents on the way home. My mom had a small pig with her and my dad had another one. She told me, "You should be ashamed, now your dad is all excited and wants to go work as a bracero with you." I spoke to my dad and he told me that it was a good idea to go and

work. My dad sent my brother to sell some animals and with that money we came here.

(Interview with Juventino Cosio 2002).

From the perspective of Mexican workers being recruited, their stories would prove to encounter difficulties regarding their recruitment experiences. Sometimes they arrived ill prepared for the time it took to get contracted; the ones that did get contracted proved to be the "lucky ones." However, the tales that I will tell of the braceros that were contracted do not reveal the stories of those who did not. Indeed, if there is a part of the story that is missing, it is of the countless number of Mexicans that did not get contracts and were turned away for various reasons. One reason was based upon not appearing to have prior experience with field work. In the example below, the potential applicants were sent away for appearing to well to do.

The people that were dressed very nicely with chains and rings were sent back. They returned one man that had a hernia, and the man that needed glasses plus the people who were dressed luxurious.

(Interview with Aldolfo Perez 2002)

Another former bracero account suggests the difference in class and educational levels among potential applicants for the program:

The first people that came here to California were not people from the fields. They were not peasants. They were people from the cities, for example Mexico City. Mexico City contracted a lot of people to come and work. There were a lot of people from different economic levels working in the fields. There were people with no education at all, some with little education, while others had a profession. There was mixture of different class levels.

(Interview with Amado Carrasco 2002)

The following stories are of the "luckiest" Mexicans who were ultimately contracted to go "Al Norte." Even among the lucky ones, there remained problems with getting access to the contracts even though the agreement between the United States and Mexico should have decreased and not increased the difficulties of contracting. Some of the stories provide further details of the abuse that Mexicans encountered while they attempted to get contracted to go north. Corruption was evident as revealed by the following interview with Don Francisco Llamas:

Paul: How many people do you think were there waiting?

Don Francisco: Thousands of people, a lot. Most of us were already sure that we were on the list and I was just waiting for the day that they would call. Some of them they would just go to see if they could get the job. Sometimes there were guys that had influence with the people who would contract us. They would give them money so that they could be on the list. In the meantime they would put us on the end of the list. They would pay to the manager of the contractors.

After making the decision to join the program, the next step was to sign up. Recruitment centers were established; the first one was in Mexico City and later in area major cities of Mexico. Braceros soon realized signing up for the program would take time and be costly. Bribes (or moridas), extra work, and exploitation of potential applicants became part of the illegal activities associated with joining the program. Signing up for the program would be the first of many discouraging problems braceros would encounter.

Recruitment Centers

For the Mexican workers looking to sign contracts, recruitment centers were found in major cities throughout Mexico. One of the first contracting centers was located in the capital city of Mexico City. It was opened in 1942; and the National Stadium in Mexico City was used to bring in thousands of Mexicans to contract. Many of the first braceros were said to have been contracted there; however, even more were said to have been turned away. Upon its opening, thousands of Mexicans anxious to join the program streamed to the capital for a chance to sign up for the program. The recruitment of braceros, however, was more difficult given the manner in which potential workers were brought to recruitment centers. Each bracero I interviewed indicated that centers within each city (i.e., Mexico City) were places where the possibility of signing a contract would occur. However, the stories of the braceros revealed how problematic it was for some braceros to obtain contracts.

One of the problems that applicants encountered was the ill-equipped nature of the process of handling a floating population. With so many potential applicants waiting to get contracted, the capital city was said to be over run by so many people and there were not enough facilities to meet their needs. As more centers began to open up, the same problems of cities ill-equipped to handle the influx of transient people was repeated. Some applicants resorted to sleeping in parks and city streets; they also searched for work and places to eat while sometimes waiting for days or weeks to get contracted:

> **Paul:** While you were waiting for the eight days, what would you do in the meantime?
>
> **Francisco:** I just would wait until they call me back.
>
> **Paul:** But the days that you were waiting, would you wait in your house?
>
> **Francisco:** No, when we were waiting we rented a room between the four of us.
>
> **Paul:** Did you work while you were waiting?
>
> **Francisco:** Yes, so we could pay for the hotel and food while we were waiting.
>
> **Paul:** Did you have money for everything?
>
> **Francisco:** Yes, we would be careful with our money so that it would last us.
>
> **Paul:** Do you remember when you stayed in the hotel, did you sleep in a bed?
>
> **Francisco:** There was no bed, we rented a room and we all slept on the floor.

Paul: There was no bed or heater?

Francisco: No, nothing like that. It was like an apartment but it was a hotel. For us coming as braceros there was nothing like that, only bathrooms so that we could be able to take a bath.

Paul: Was it hard to come?

Francisco: Yes, but when you are young you don't feel nothing.

Paul: Where would you guys eat?

Francisco: They would sell food in the streets, that's where we would eat. There was a lot of little businesses that we could choose from.

Paul: Tacos?

Francisco: Yes, tacos, they were the cheapest.

Paul: So you lived in a hotel and ate in the streets?

Francisco: The food stands were near by where the braceros would stay. The food stands were there for the braceros because we were the only ones that would go there to eat.

(Interview with Francisco Llamas 2002)

A former bracero's second recruitment process describes the problems of other potential braceros who could not afford the cost of shelter such as a hotel room:

Since we did not know anyone there, we had to rent a room because hotels were expensive. From there we went to the offices and signed up for the program. If people were lucky enough they would leave the following day. People who could not afford a place to sleep often slept and ate on the streets. Street vendors often sold food for cheap prices.

(Interview with Benjamin Munoz 2002)

Frequently, braceros described how local townspeople began to help them. With thousands of men waiting to be contracted, and with few resources, it was not uncommon to see men in the streets waiting for their chance at being contracted. As a result, some community members often lent a hand to potential applicants by offering them food, shelter, and work to help them get by:

Paul: How did people feed themselves?

Don Jesus: Well, those who knew people in Hermosillo ate at their houses. There were also people of good heart that fed others. Depending on the situation, many people lasted more than others did. Once you ran out of money, you were forced to return to your hometown. Things were not so expensive but if you ran out of money that did not matter. Money was worth more back then.

(Interview with Jesus Saceudo 2002)

Following the increased number of workers needed, it soon became necessary to open more contracting centers throughout Mexico. In Guadalajara, Irapuato, Tampico, Hermosillo, Empalme, and Monterey recruiting centers opened to ease the problems of contracting applicants. The centers attracted thousands of Mexican; in most cases, the cities were ill-equipped to handle the large floating population of recruits. Some just gave up hope of being selected and returned to their homes. Those lucky enough to be selected knew it came at a price.

> *When contractors began contracting people, the local town government informed the surrounding towns. It was also informed through the newspaper or the radio. All the information concerning date, town, and hour was given for braceros to attend. At times we had to go to the local municipal townhouse or at times contractors were stationed at army camps. On December of 1951, I found out that contractors were coming to my town. It was actually one of my compadres that informed me about the contractors at Irapuato. I decided to go and register. When I got to the army camp, there were lines everywhere. There were a total of four lines. The wait was going to take a while, but I decided to stay because I was eager to register. . . . I was very lucky I got into the program. I got cuts from one of the persons standing in line so I would not have to go to the end of the line. I'm not lying to you; the man that gave me cuts, which was then behind me, was the last person to get hired. I was very lucky. Contractors only took twenty from every line. I was very happy and looked forward to coming to the U.S.*
>
> (Interview with Refugio"Cuco" Gonzalez 2002)

Once at the centers, the recruits were asked information about their health. Risks of being turned away were genuine. Having any physical disabilities would make it highly likely you would not be chosen. Recruited in 1943, Don Florentino Palacio describes his selection process:

> *They examined you to see if you were sick or not; there were doctors there to examine you. They checked your body and eyes. My other brother had colored eyes and the doctor said he couldn't enter. My brother got upset and said, "I know how to read better than you, give me a newspaper and I'll read it for you." . . . He wanted to prove his reading skills to the doctor. The doctor gave him the newspaper and the doctor was astonished at the fact that he could read really well. He said, "Ok, pass."*
>
> (Interview with Florentino Palacio 2002)

When I met Don Florentino Palacio, his health was poor. He lived with his daughter and son-in-law in Santa Barbara. He, like other elderly braceros depend on their families to see them through their remaining years. Years later, I returned to visit them and inquire about his health. Unfortunately, Don Florentino Palacio had passed away. His story revealed the recruiting process of the early members of the program. My interview with Don Florentino Palacio included the lack of information about what work he would be assigned and little about the 10 percent deduction:

Don Florentino: No, it was a very big hall. They made you get undressed to check you. You could only get in if you were healthy.

Paul: When you signed the contract, did they explain everything to you? How many months, how much they would pay you?

Don Florentino: No, over there we were not told anything, you were just contracted and sent. They sent you to different places. You were not told what you were going to do, nor what you would work in. They just sent you.

Paul: Do you remember when you signed that they would take away 10 percent from you?

Don Florentino: Yes, you signed and were not told where you would work. It said that they would take it. They would have to claim the other 10 percent back in Mexico.

Another interview with a former bracero in Santa Barbara revealed a similar peek into the recruitment center. The process was not at all fixed for the benefit of braceros, but to get them in and out if they passed the physical requirements of the program:

Paul: Did you know what the type of work you were going to do as a bracero and what city you were going to be placed in?

Don Alejandro: No because the program consisted of being brought to this country for the purpose of working. Even though I did not have experience working in the fields, I gave it my best to come and work in this country. If one has the will to do work, one tries harder to succeed. . . . We had to pass a medical exam, which consisted of a physical. If we passed the exam, then we were in the program. The headquarters were held at Mexico's National Soccer Stadium.

Paul: Was there a lot of people at the stadium?

Don Alejandro: Yes, there was a lot of people and the majority were from Mexico City. I did not see any peasants there during this time. First they checked your hands, which in order to pass the exam they had to see whether you had calluses or not. Before taking the physical, what I did was, I got a rock and scrubbed my hands, making them look rough.

Paul: Were the physicians that examined you Mexican or Americans?

Don Alejandro: They were both Mexican and American, half-and-half.

Paul: At what time did examinations take place?

Don Alejandro: Examinations took place in the morning.

Paul: How long did they last?

Don Alejandro: They lasted approximately three to four hours.

Paul: Were you shown your results right after?

Don Alejandro: No, we had to wait a whole week to find out.

(Interview with Alejandro Gomez 2002)

Overall, two million braceros were recruited—most in the interior of Mexico. The border also became a site where braceros were sent to renew their contracts rather than going all the way back into Mexico. One can argue that recruitment of guest workers is not a science and is difficult to do. However, considering what these workers had to give up in order to join the program, more thought could have been put into the process. Indeed, Ernesto Garlarza was correct that the bracero program was a managed form of immigration. But from its beginning to its ending in 1964, Mexicans who went through the program found it inherently plagued with unresolved recruiting problems.

Bracero Narratives and Recruitment

Most, if not all, of the braceros I interviewed heard about the program prior to going to the recruitment centers. From their villages to the urban areas where they had to go to sign up for the program, you get a sense that the program offered them the opportunity to work. The story of one of the braceros I interviewed involved the loss of his wife prior to his contracting to come to the United States as a bracero. His wife died tragically due to her appendix erupting and having no possible means to rush to a local hospital for help. He says of his contracting experience:

> Well, my father did not tell me anything or stop me from coming. We used to work in agriculture but after I heard about the Bracero Program, I knew it was a big opportunity for me. At the time, I was not making enough to support my family with the job I was doing. The products that we harvested were not worth much. I remember harvesting pinto beans, corn, wheat, and peanuts. Peanuts was the product that we cultivated the most because it was worth more that the other products. At the end of the harvest, buyers used to come and buy it from us. Even townspeople bought peanuts from us. It was a very popular product in the town. After finding out about the program, I told my dad about this great opportunity. From what I know, the U.S. government requested Mexican workers and both countries agreed on the program. I came with the thought in mind of helping my family. I, along with one of my brothers, decided to come together.

> (Interview with Agustin Alamanza 2002)

One former bracero recounts his experience of being recruited:

> Yeah, it was in the middle of May or by the end of May. I found this friend and he told me, "Let's go to the United States," and I told him, "No, what are we going to do over there?" and he told me, "Well they are having contracts in Mexico City.". . . And I told him, "Then you are not going over there" because he had a good job. I asked him, "What are you going to do over there, you have a good job?" and he told me, "Well I want to go and see how it is over there. If you do not believe me, tomorrow at 6:30 in the morning go to the train station. The train is leaving at that time and I am leaving too." I got exited too and I decided to go to see if I got hired. He told me to meet him at the train station in the morning and he took two other people. I asked him if he

was leaving after all and he told me, "Yes." So I told him I was going too. I quit my job and we left in the train.

We left on a Monday and we got to Mexico City on Tuesday. We stayed in a hotel. There were four of us and we got two rooms, two people per each room. The next day, we woke up early and we went to get information about the contracts. We got there and we started to fill out papers and we had to wait to take a physical exam. We were there almost the whole day because we were going with a bunch of doctors. They told us that we did not complete everything, so we had to go the next day and finish filling out the papers. It was a Thursday, when we finished filling out the papers and on Friday we had an appointment in a stadium, because there was a lot of people.

All of us were in the stadium in Mexico City and they told us how to behave there. First of all, the benefits that we were going to have and that they were going to have us here, and that we were going to have medical services and that they were going to take 10 percent off to put it the National Bank of Mexico. In case we did not save any money, we were going to be able to take out money from the bank to go back to our land where we belonged.

That was on Friday, and on Monday at six in the morning we were in the Buena Vista Station. There we were going to know which ones passed the test and were in good condition to see if we got a contract. We woke up early; we took a cab and we went to the Buena Vista Station. There were a lot of people. We all got in line. The four of us were going together—the ones that came with me from Apatzingan. I saw how they moved an old man from the line. Then my other friend he went straight to the train. . . . And I was next and I went straight too. Then the next one was put on the side; he was young, 20 years old. The rest of them did not get a contract because they did not have good health. From the four of us, only two of us got the contract. We were there on Monday till 4 pm when we took the bus to come here. We passed through a lot of towns and wherever we stopped the people were yelling, "Why are you going over there? Don't go, they are going to kill you over there."

(Interview with Amado Carrasco 2002)

Once the recruitment process had been started, the choice of which men to be chosen was based on finding those with prior field hand experience. Mexicans without prior experience would resort to roughing their hands in order to appear that they had prior field hand experience. Here is one former braceros account:

Yeah. They would check your entire body. After they had finish checking my whole entire body they let you through and give you a paper that said that you are now ready to go. People were already put into groups and were ready to leave. From there we would leave on a train. Everyone that had pass the exam would get on the train and leave.

(Interview with Blas Torino 2003)

Other experiences suggested that getting to the initial line for recruitment would prove difficult. Some had to provide labor before they could expect to be picked for the program. For example, government officials would expect potential recruits to work for them and that would serve the way for them to be picked or put on a list to be chosen.

> Well, I had to first work in Obregon picking cotton. I believe we had to pick one thousands kilos in order to receive a letter. I remember leaving my house in June and was able to get hired in October after picking my share of the cotton. I returned in December to once again see those waiting in line to get hired.
>
> (Interview with Salvador Munoz 2002).

One other difficulty confronted by potential recruits was the lack of temporary housing for those waiting to become part of the program. Many waiting for their opportunity to get access to the recruitment process were either too poor to pay for housing or ran out of money. This former bracero recalls his experience having to wait numerous days (while waiting in Monterey) before he was selected:

> I did not know if I had to wait for five days or one day, I did not know. I was lucky that I only had to wait for five days. There were people that had to wait there for a month or two and they had no money and they were dirty, etc. When we got contracted we knew that we were going to start working in one or two days.
> . . . There were days that they took a lot of people. Sometimes buses would arrive and the people on those buses would leave right away. It took us five days of waiting and we would sleep wherever we could. . . . On the streets, and when I had money I got to sleep in a hotel, if not I would sleep on the street floors on top of a cardboard. . . . The streets were full of people sleeping there. Whoever had money to pay for a hotel, they paid for it. Another thing that they used to do also was to rent a room in a house and ten to twenty people would sleep there.
>
> (Interview with Miguel Cuevas 2002)

Other former braceros commented on the lack of securing shelter while waiting to be contracted. After a period of time, entire communities began to recognize the impact of the program and began to provide shelter or offer food.

> **Paul:** While you were waiting, I'm sure you met a lot of people. I'm also sure that you had the money to pay for a hotel. But what happened to people that did not have the money to rent hotels?
>
> **Don Jesus:** They slept on the streets or at parks. After we ran out of money, we stayed at a park. It was hot weather and we did not need any blankets. We slept on the floors looking like a camp with all the people camping at parks. Local businesses remained open because they knew that money was coming in some way or another. Businesses just sprang out of nowhere.
>
> **Paul:** How many people slept at the park every night?

Don Jesus: Thousands of people slept there. Well, they not only slept in parks. They also slept in homes if they were given a chance to do so. You could sleep anywhere in town.

(Interview with Jesus Saceudo 2002)

Conclusion

The recruitment stories revealed in this chapter reflect the initial step for former braceros who are now permanent settlers in the United States. Now, as settled immigrants, they deserve to be recognized for their contributions and sacrifices. This chapter revealed the inherent problems recruiting guest workers. Whether ill-prepared to handle the number of recruits or unable to handle the amount of potential applicants at one time, many of the stories revealed the hardships endured. Many potential recruits were either turned away for health reasons or for not being able to stay long enough to secure a contract. The recruitment process only begins to touch upon the Bracero Program experience among former recruits. If you were chosen to enter the program, the next stage was just the beginning of further hardships they encountered.

Indeed, once recruited, the workers would have to endure the next step, the trip north to the border or *frontera*. The recruitment stories revealed in this chapter reflect the problems associated with the recruitment process of immigrant guest workers. Whether ill prepared to handle the number of recruits or unable to offer a fair contracting experience, many of the stories revealed the hardships of the recruitment process. Once recruited, however, the workers would have to endure the next step. The trip north to the border, then being selected by growers, and finally the trip in the interior of the United States. Former braceros were proud to do the work requested of them. Despite the harsh realities of getting recruited, former braceros recall reapplying. Don Lamberto Garcia who I interviewed in Oxnard, California retells his second recruiting experience:

> After I went back to Mexico and was contracted again in Monterey. I had the money to pay again. This time we were charged $200 pesos for registration. We paid and went to Monterey and took a week to get hired. To tell you the truth, we even slept on the streets. We didn't have a place to go. The next time we were hired, we entered through Reinosa and worked close to San Juan.

(Interview with Lamberto Garcia 2002)

After going through the process the first time, the recruitment process was often made easier as their bosses often encouraged them to re-sign up. Re-signing sometimes did not mean having to return to Mexico. Growers would go out of their way to keep them. In the case below, Don Refugio "Cuco" Gonzalez describes how his boss at the ranch where he worked secured legal papers:

> When I completed their paperwork, it was because the company helped me. Also, the company at Dos Pueblos took care of my immigration status. Most of my contracts were for sixty days and I had to return to Mexico every December.

---

[3] Last name was changed to protect the identity of the person.

[4] First name was changed to protect the identity of the person.

I was only able to come back and forth when work was available. When I picked up my last check, I asked Munoz[3] for a letter of recommendation which I still have. Munoz spoke to Chuck[4] and Chuck gave me instead a letter that would help me legalize my immigration status. It was good for six months.

(Interview with "Cuco" Gonzalez 2002)

Despite the semblance of keeping the recruitment process in some kind of order, there were countless numbers of potential recruits who for various reasons were exploited or simply denied the opportunity to become part of the Bracero Program. Cities where the recruitments occurred were often overwhelmed with too many Mexicans willing to participate. With little in the way of being able to feed and house the migrating population, many often had to secure shelter and food on the streets. Shelter would sometimes mean sleeping on the streets where they could find a place to stay at night. Public parks served as possible overnight sleeping quarters or simply sleeping on the streets with the hope of not being robbed or assaulted.

In short, the recruitment process was flawed. Increased oversight of the process was needed but never provided. Some potential recruits had to travel many miles just for the chance of being selected. They left families behind and sometimes spent what they had brought with them. The cost alone was an expense. Potential recruits would have to resort to finding temporary work. Resorting to what was available, potential recruits would share rooms. There were few options if the recruitment process was slowed for whatever reason. A former bracero describes his experience below:

No, the people that had money would stay in hotels. But people that didn't have money like most of us would stay in things that looked like porches and that's where we stayed. You could see all the people just dropping to the floor. Then it started to rain. The porches only cover the water from the top not the bottom. So during those moments everyone just stood up. People really suffered during that time. People that had brought money with them didn't really suffer because they could just go and buy a hotel room.

(Interview with Blas Torino 2003)

Recruitment is the first and most important step toward initializing repeat migration. Once the *pioneer* migrant has experienced the depth of migrating alone, a second migration experience is therefore possible. For braceros whose work was valued by growers an additional opportunity to sign another contract occurred. Countless studies have recorded this method of growers willing to keep braceros after their contracts expired (Gonzalez and Fernadez, 2003; Durand, Massey, and Parrado, 1999).

CHAPTER 3

The Journey North

Former bracero recalling his boarding of the train to take him north to the U.S-Mexico border:

. . . I came by myself and I was twenty. I had to have confidence. From Guadalajara, Calexico. I left on a Sunday at noon, and I got there Tuesday at 8 am. I got there on a train, which had both people and cargo. It stopped at several cities, and it was slow; I was very bored. I was sad because there were two lines. The man that chose people, there were two hundred of us, he would say "you" and "you." He mostly chose young men. He picked me and I came to Santa Barbara. What I didn't like is that he chose only the young ones. I felt sad taking the jobs of older men who had families.
(Interview with Ulbaldo Coronel 2002)

Growing up in Santa Barbara, California, I took for granted the treasure of a town it is. Today it's more of a tourist town than I recall growing up. Indeed, it is visited, or has become the home residence, by Hollywood stars Kevin Costner and Oprah. Every August there is the *Old Spanish Days* celebration.[1] For about one week being Latino is a good thing. I've seen my own

---

[1] It is also called Fiesta days. A local resident is chosen to serve as Marshall to host the events at the Spanish Mission church and the Spanish style court house.

daughters, Saundra and AnnaAlicia, dance in parades and other events during *Old Spanish Days*. In addition, my two nieces, Christina and Selena Castaneda, grew up from toddlers to adult women dancing for one of the local dance studios. My son James, and nephew Stephen Castaneda, spent fiesta days plotting ways to crack the confetti eggs, sold at the mercardos,[2] on their sisters who had to remain perfectly dressed for their performances. Throughout those years, my father would film his granddaughters participating in the parades and dance performances. In short, Old Spanish Days celebration has become a López and Castaneda family tradition.

However, as a long time former local resident,[3] you begin to question what *Spanish Days* means. In my view *Old Spanish Days* is the privatizing of a culture, rather than viewing the historical significance of the colonization period embedded in the town's history. Commercialization of former Spanish colonization is the emphasis of the week-long event, which further enhances the pocketbooks of local store owners and vendors. Throughout the year, Santa Barbara attracts tourists from around the world. It is one of the most unique communities along the Southern California Coast. Although a general agreement between the local community and Chumash tribe has been agreed upon, there is still an ahistorical approach to the colonization of Native Americans by the local media and townsfolk (McWilliams, 1975). Few people are reminded during the week-long celebration that the Spaniards enslaved the Chumash tribe in Santa Barbara as part of the California mission system. In order to control the Chumash, the priest used religion to convert them into "civilized" individuals. The once proud Chumash were exploited as chattel workers according to historical accounts (Pitt, 1966). The few remaining reminders of the Chumash culture are the shell-like adobe buildings now seen by tourists.

In today's economic climate, for working class folks in Santa Barbara, the purchasing of a home is out of their reach. It's a great place to visit but unless you come packed with tons of cash to spend, good luck finding a home within a purchaseable price range. For example, my parents are retired now, and they bought their home in 1964. The price of the home was about $26,000. The monthly mortgage payment was just over a hundred dollars a month. Today, that same house is valued close to $2 million. My parents were able to make the final payment on the house in the 1980s. Both my parents worked until they retired and are now modestly keeping themselves busy. Rather than buy one of the new tract homes, my parents purchased the home from someone who built homes on what has turned out to be an upscale area. Occasionally, from my parent's front window you can see a stretch limo going further up the canyon road. My dad completed high school in Mexico and my mom dropped out of high school before completing her senior year. Recently, my dad and mom revealed to everyone that they had eloped. To the chagrin of her brothers (she was the only sister) and the rest of

---

[2] Known in English as local stores.

[3] I was born and raised in Santa Barbara, but after attending college in Los Angeles I was never able to financially afford to remain. But on visits to see my family I have seen the changes to my beloved city. I'm not a tourist when I go back to Santa Barbara. I feel much at home when I stay with my parents. Most of the changes to the community within the last twenty years have been the polarization of high-end workers and low-end workers.

her family the elopement didn't go over very well. Needless to say, they have been married over fifty years.

My father retired from the city of Santa Barbara as a custodian. I can still hear his old red Ford truck warming up around 5 a.m. The overnight dew would make the old Ford truck hard to start each morning. He would start the truck and let it warm up while attending to the last few things he needed to do. Usually it was to make his lunch. My mom would catch the local city bus to work. To catch the bus, my mother had to walk only one block to Milpas Street. After my dad retired, I could recall having him take my mom to work after she missed the bus. After she got home from work, my dad reminded her to be on time. Although she tried vigilantly, she always seemed to miss it at least once during the week. They are quite a pair.

I retell this story since I remember how it was to be part of a working class family. I didn't have much when I was growing up. But my parents provided more than enough of what I needed. I learned the value of taking care of my belongings; indeed, from washing my car once a week or keeping my kitchen clean. I am more vigilant now as I am divorced and live alone. Although my parents were both born in the United States, they lived their lives similar to the ones experienced by Mexican immigrants. As mentioned from an earlier chapter, they began their marital life in the early 1950s—the *Mexican American* generation as Chicano historian Mario T. Garcia has labeled that period.

The ability of non-Mexicans to distinguish the difference between Mexican Americans and Mexicans was surely to their disadvantage. I think my parents did their best to hide the ill effects of being Mexican toward their three children by outsiders. The cultural gap between being Mexican and Mexican American during my parent's marriage is evident. As Chicano historian George J. Sanchez (1995) examined in his book *Becoming Mexican American*, my parents also experienced the cultural divide. To this day I would argue that they are caught between the values of their parents as Mexican immigrants and their children's cultural evolution as Chicana/os. Similar to Sanchez's examination of wanting to know more about his parents' earlier life, I wanted to draw upon my parents' life to record the migration of Mexican braceros. From the stories I've been told, my grandparents migrated north to the United States during the early part of the twentieth century. My paternal grandparents returned to Mexico in the 1930s. My maternal grandparents separated and divorced when my mother was young. I recall spending my youth with my mom's mother, but I don't recall spending much time with my mom's father.

Both my parents were born in the United States. Both sets of my grandparents were born in Mexico. My dad spent his youth in Mexico and came back as a *cultural hybrid* of both countries. With few exceptions, migrating to a new country is a remarkable transformation to undertake. Leaving a familiar place behind can be life transforming. For immigrants, it can involve leaving family behind and experiencing a country that is unfamiliar—or even hostile. The view that immigrants find the United States an inviting place is based upon a myth. Countless documentation of immigrants experiencing anxiety or despair has been documented (Chavez, 2008; Sanchez, 1995). Feeling anxious about their decision to migrate is not limited to Mexican immigrants. Indeed, historian Ronald Takaki's examination (1989) of Asian migration to Hawaii and the West Coast illuminates the problem. As one former bracero explained his initial experience in the United States, life was difficult to adjust to:

> *. . . Nothing was simple, as it seemed. Some of us did not know how to pick cotton, while others did not know how to spray pesticides. This type of work was way different than any type of work we had ever done. Food was also different; we had never had this type of food in our lives. We had to get up really early in the morning, eat breakfast, which most of the time consisted of oatmeal, toast and eggs and then we headed off to work. The rancheros would be waiting for you early. We also had to do our laundry, which I had never done in my life. Everything was new to me and I had to learn, knowing that I was hundreds of miles away from my home. It was sad at times; some became medically sick, while others became homesick.*
>
> (Interviewed with Jesus Saucedo 2002)

Following the passing of medical exams and acquiring the legal papers to enter the program, braceros were swiftly boarded on trains or buses. For some braceros coming north to the United States, the trip was their first time. Some were extremely excited about the event. Others were apprehensive about what to expect. Don Ubaldo Coronel explains his experience as a young nineteen-year-old traveling to the state of Missouri:[4]

Paul: What were you thinking while on your way to Missouri?

Don Ubaldo: Well, I kept calm because I was riding with relatives. However, in my mind I kept telling myself that I was not going to return the next time. I was young at the time and expected better. I had so many dreams of nice houses and good work. I wanted to work in a pueblo and not a ranch. The trip also added to my discomfort. The whole way we saw darkness and heard rain and thunder at night.

This chapter examines the trip north to the border. The accounts place the migration of braceros into a virtual experience. Risking everything, they hoped to accomplish what they were unable to do in Mexico. Depending upon the time it took from the recruitment center to the border, braceros faced uncomfortable seating, food that was not appetizing, no bathroom facilities on trains, and other less desirable conditions. Once contracted and aboard the transportation provided little choice but for them to endure the trip. Contracted and boarded on trains or buses to the border, this was the initial process of what would turn out to be a long-term settlement process. The organizers of the agreement did not anticipate the long-term factors despite previous recruitment efforts during the early part of the twentieth century of Mexican immigrants (Garlarza, 1964; Garcia, 1982).

Previous examinations of braceros traveling north to the border are largely historical accounts (Driscoll, 1999; Garlarza, 1964; Calvatta, 1992; Gamboa, 2000; Craig, 1971). Lacking in these previous analyses is the human side of migration. Indeed, the interviews that follow are a mixture of personal acquaintances and research contacts. For some braceros, migrating north

---

[4] The term Don is a title employed to show respect or honor before a man's first name.

to the United States was an unknown experience. For others, it was a chance to return after multiple visits. Don Benjamin Munoz who first came in 1951 explains his second trip north:

> **Paul:** Did you come in a train again?
>
> **Don Benjamin:** Yes, we came in a train once again, had the same food as the previous year, and went through the same inspections we had gone through the year before. We were happy to come once again. It was actually better this time because we knew what to expect and sometimes we saw the same people again. We arrived in Ciudad Juarez, crossed the border, and went to El Paso and from there to Seminole.

(Interview with Benjamin Munoz 2003)

Only after being picked by growers did braceros get some idea of their destination. Don Amado Carrasco, who I interviewed in 2003, turned out to be the father of two daughters who attended Our Lady of Guadalupe School. His youngest daughter was a former classmate of my sister. He would end up in Santa Barbara after his second contract experience: Below he describes his experience:

> . . . We took the bus to the border. There were several different lines for those who were about to cross pertaining to different times as well. There was a line with people who had contracts. We went to that line and there was a "boss" waiting for us. We got there and they concentrated on people from different parts of Mexico. When I got to the center, I saw what I just told you. That was it. Then we got on the bus and we drove all the way to Santa Maria. On the way there, we lost the three guys because at the border they asked you where you wanted to go. We said we wanted to go to California.

(Interview with Amado Carrasco 2003)

Don Benjamin Munoz describes what happened to him upon his first trip to the border. His family's prior experience with coming to the United States eased his first trip. He told me that his father had come to the United States as far back as the 1920s. Below, Don Benjamin talks about his first trip to the border:

> Once we got to the border, groups were sent with certain braceros to different places. We first arrived at La Mesa and from there we were taken to Las Cruces to pick cotton. At our arrival at Las Cruces, the rancheros gave us money to buy food, however, once we started working we had to buy our own food.

(Interview with Benjamin Munoz 2004)

Multiple contracts signed by braceros were not uncommon. Don Salvador Munoz was contracted more than once. He explained how he continued to be contracted. In this case he first went to Texas, then Nebraska, and ended up in Kansas.

> We left El Paso on a bus and arrived the next day in Dallas. As soon as we got there we ate and then boarded another bus to Nebraska. I worked in Nebraska, and that same year I signed up once again for the contract there in Nebraska, and from there I was sent to work in Kansas. We were told to go

to a local church where sign ups where taking place. Upon arriving at the church, other braceros and I got in line and were asked what type of work we had previously done. I told them what vegetables and fruits I had picked and so forth. They were satisfied with what I had done and rehired me to work in Kansas. The contract was a one-year contract and that same day we boarded a bus provided by the company and arrived early morning in Kansas.

(Interview with Salvador Munoz 2002)

Multiple contract signings not only helped to ease their migration, but also provided familiarity with the United States and the potential for settlement. Don Refugio "Cuco" Gonzalez, who is now settled permanently, recalls arriving in Santa Barbara:

. . . I was around twenty-two years old when I came as a bracero and got a ninety-day contract here in Santa Barbara. That contract ended and they gave us another one; a government representative would sign the contract. That's how it went for me, renewing [contracts] because I wanted to be here [in the U.S.]. We had everything, we had a place to sleep and eat and our bosses didn't charge us when we couldn't work so I would send all my money [back home]. I kept renewing my contract until the day came when they told us that there would be no more contracts and that the government had changed. They told us that everyone was to leave. I like this country a lot so I asked if I could get a recommendation so if there was to be another [Bracero Program] I could be contracted at the same place again. They gave me a card that was good for six months.

(Interview with Refugio "Cuco" Gonzalez, 2002)

According to historian Gilberto Gonzalez, countless recruits never made it past the border. Rejected at the border, recruits were sent back over the border and had to go back home at their own expense. Border cities were overpopulated with rejected recruits with no jobs and no money (Gonzalez, 2007). Gonzalez had this to say about those rejected:

Each year one of every six men who entered the El Centro Reception Center was dismissed for a variety of reasons. Many thousands of unfortunate men were sent back across the border to Mexicali with bus fare to return to Empalme.

(Gonzalez, 2007)

Waiting at the border to be selected could be another chance of being returned. Other braceros simply had to wait their turns at the border, get re-examined for lice or venereal disease, and then were taken to their destinations. Braceros with prior experience with the recruitment process would sometimes switch their destinations by boarding trains taking them to better work sites.

Now, as elderly and retired workers, they no longer have the anxieties they experienced during their contracted days. Indeed, speaking with them decades after their migration as braceros, there is a sense of peace of mind regarding their settlement in the United States.[5] With extended family members living in the United States or Mexico, these former braceros no longer view the United States as a foreign country, but rather as an adopted country due to the amount of time that has passed. With children and grandchildren in the United States, it is difficult for them to separate their bracero migration and their current status as elderly men. At some point you begin to take the next step. In this case, these former braceros are settled and living their twilight years as former guest workers and now as settled first generation Americans.

Al Norte

If they had money to buy food, braceros traveling north to the border would buy food along the way. For some that was not a problem, while others who had no extra money would have to wait till their next meal. Those without money would find their next meal only when they arrived at the labor camps. Don Paulino Pacheco did not hold back when describing his border crossing:

> We were taken in carrier trains. They almost looked like animal cages. A bucket full of water was placed in the middle of the wagon, but we had nowhere to use the bathroom. The train passed through the desert into Mexicali. All we had to eat was a piece of bread and water. Nothing else was provided. When we arrived in Mexicali, we were taken to what looked like a warehouse; we were stripped from our clothes, and they were sprayed with different disinfectants.
>
> (Interview with Paulino Pacheco 2002)

Once on the trains or buses, braceros were exposed for the first time to American food. Most of them were not upset to see that tacos or other forms of Mexican food were not served to them. Rather, unfamiliar American food was the common food served to them. Here a former bracero describes what he was given to eat:

> It was Mexican workers that worked on the train and served the food. For lunch we had a bologna sandwich, a soda, and fruit.
>
> (Interview with Benjamin Munoz 2003)

Don Jesus Saucedo describes the train ride and the food given to him and the other braceros. Faced with not eating, the American sandwich was their only source of food. The impression of the food appears to have stayed with him after all the years that have since passed. Don Jesus Saucedo describes his encounter with American cuisine:

> **Paul:** How long was the train ride from Guanajuato to Texas?
>
> **Don Jesus:** It took about two days and then when we went to San Louis, Missouri.
>
> **Paul:** And all you had to eat was a sandwich per day?
>
> **Don Jesus:** Well they would buy sandwiches along that way. We ate three sandwiches a day along with a soda. However, we as Mexicans were not

---

5 Deborah Cohen's analysis of former Mexican braceros from Durango, Mexico cites the ease at which they now talk about their former days as guest workers. The title of her forthcoming book is *Transnational Subjects*.

used to eating that type of food. We did not have any other option but to eat it because we were hungry. It was the first time we got to see and taste American food; bologna, cheese, tomatoes, etc. They would give us coffee with a sandwich in the morning. Every time I eat a sandwich it brings back memories of those days.

Below, a conversation with Don Sacramento Jimenez reveals how it was for him:

Paul: When you were in the train did they stop to give you something to eat?

Don Sacramento: No more food. If you had the money, you could buy food. But if you did not have money, you would not eat.

Paul: Do you remember if most of the Braceros had money?

Don Sacramento: Most of us did not have money. When I came in the train that time, I had 20 cents (Mexican). The money I earned working while I got my contract, I spent it all while I was working because I had to buy food every day. The day I came I only had the sandwich they gave me and my 20 cents.

Paul: What did you do?

Don Sacramento: I could not do anything. I just did not eat. Even if you were hungry, what could you do? We knew that we had the contract. We got to El Centro, California.

I interviewed a bracero through my brother-in-law's friend from high school which illustrated the racial divide. Racial discrimination was not tolerated; yet time after time, braceros encountered discrimination. Indeed, since the passing of the *Plessey Ferguson Act* of 1896, racial discrimination toward Blacks, Mexicans, and other persons of color was mandated by the state. The law did state, *separate but equal,* but there was never anything equal when it came to the schools that minority children attended compared to the schools whites attended. Jim Crow laws made certain that persons of color were treated unfairly. Besides inadequate schools for children, adults endured segregation in housing, at restaurants, on public buses, and in restrooms. As a result, braceros were being brought into a country that, for many decades, had already established a racial barrier between whites and non-whites.

On the way to the U.S., especially in Denver, the toilets were not washed at all and the smell was disgusting. We were not allowed to go into the station's bathrooms, forcing us to use the train's toilets. To top it off, there was a sign prohibiting Blacks and Mexicans to use the toilets. The same thing happened in Montana and Riverside, California. In Riverside, there was a line for Blacks and Mexicans and one for whites. Most of the time I had to sneak in the white folk's line. This also happened in restaurants. But I always worked my way around lines.

(Interview with Reynaldo Aceves 2003)

The racial divide was also experienced by other former braceros who encountered other racial groups who felt threatened by their presence. As one former bracero describes his time in the

South, African Americans did not like seeing Mexican immigrant workers and this led to physical confrontations. Indeed, a former bracero describes what they encountered:

> There were no opportunities for anyone. Not even for Mexicans, forcing them to work in the fields. Not even restaurants would hire (Mexicans) until the end of the war. After the war, many people were employed. I got to see discrimination against people of color. They would have to go to the far end of the bus. On Greyhound buses there were two bathrooms, one for whites and one for people of color. The same kind of discrimination also existed in Sacramento between Filipinos and Anglos.
>
> (Interviewed with Alex Ayala 2002)

Don Jose Gonzales first told me that discrimination toward Mexicans was not a problem. But later in the discussion he admitted to seeing discriminating evidence.

> **Paul:** When you were in Pennsylvania, did you go to other parts of the city?
>
> **Don Jose:** No, well the town was a tourist town.
>
> **Paul:** Did you go to the theater, or out dancing?
>
> **Don Jose:** At that time we were not allowed into a lot of places.
>
> **Paul:** Why?
>
> **Don Jose:** Discrimination, the Black people had their colonies, and the Italians had their own colonies, and Americans, we were not sold anything. Everything was segregated.
>
> **Paul:** So, did you go to the theater?
>
> **Don Jose:** No, well we did not understand anything, why go? Dances, well sometimes there were Mexican dances, but very few.

El Train

Braceros I interviewed spoke of the train as the most familiar form of transportation. Depending how far they were from the U.S. border, the trip could take less than a day or several days. As guest workers it was likely assumed they should feel happy to be contracted and on their way to earn money in the United States. However, I wanted to know how accommodating the train ride was, especially among those who had to travel for more than few days just to reach the border. The braceros did not expect to ride in first-class accommodations; but at least seats that would be enough to sleep in should have been provided. Here are some examples of the conditions experienced:

> **Paul:** Did you also sleep in the train? Were beds or seats provided?
>
> **Don Jesus:** Yes, we had to sleep on the train floor either sitting or lying down. They never took us to hotels to spend the night. They did not have any consideration for us. Well, they had no funds to bring us first class. We never had those types of privileges.

Every semester, I find that one of my students' relatives was a former bracero. A former bracero who I met through one of my students at Chico State spoke of the conditions on the train. Even though he entered toward the end of the program, the condition of the trains remained inadequate. Don Francisco describes the train and what sort of sitting and sleeping arrangements were provided:

Paul: Do you remember what the train was like?

Don Francisco: It was a cargo train where instead of seats it was four pieces of wood. You didn't have anywhere to lean, you were just sitting. It was a little bad transportation place.

Paul: Was it just braceros?

Don Francisco: It looked like there were people traveling too.

Paul: Was it hot in there?

Don Francisco: Yes, because it was late and there was no air conditioner.

Paul: Did you have water?

Don Francisco: No, when the train stopped we would get off and buy water or soda.

Paul: Were you able to sleep in the train?

Don Francisco: No, there was nowhere to sleep on. It was a 2 by 12 inch table like and that was it.

Paul: Were there bathrooms?

Don Francisco: No, when the train stopped we would just get off and go anywhere around there. In the morning before getting on everyone went to the bathroom.

Paul: When you got to the border how were you?

Don Francisco: All dirty once we go to Mexicali.

My interview with Don Jose Para-Ramos took place in Ojai, California. His boss contacted me. His boss found my research project online and wanted to be a part of the project. This interview illustrates how former braceros become attached to their bosses. It was clear his boss knew much about Don Jose Para-Ramos's family in Mexico and why he continued to work in the United States. I wanted to know about how his train ride from Mexico to the border had gone. At the time of my interview he was sixty-eight years old and still working in Ojai.

Paul: How was it when you were on the train?

Don Jose: Most of the time they would treat us as cargo. It was very difficult. If we wanted to sleep, we had to sitting down; and if we wanted to go to the bathroom, everyone had to hold hands...that way we could go to the bathroom. When you came from Mexico to United States, they would put you in as cargo, but when you came from the United States to Mexico they would put you in passenger seats.

One cannot say the provided transportation benefited braceros. I would argue the need for getting braceros as quickly to the fields or work site far outweighed their comfort. Evidence of this is provided by multiple sources. The accounts vary, but generally speaking travel from the border to the work site was inadequate. In the following exchange with Don Alex Ayala, he describes his trip from the border and how it was not very difficult. Skilled as a mechanic he repaired a tractor:

> When we arrived at El Paso, the train was almost empty. From the 800 only about 600 remained. It was a comfortable trip. We did not come in those so-called carrier trains. We never experienced what other braceros experienced. We never got sprayed with disinfectants or were our heads shaven. Nothing like that ever happened. We were treated as tourists. I'm telling you the truth. . . . We rode all night and arrived the next day in Sacramento around 3 p.m. In Sacramento a group of women was waiting for us playing different types of music. The government was confused because it expected poor farm workers in sandals when instead what it got was a wave of city people. I was telling my daughter a while ago that we all came from the city. In that group there was only one peasant that we named "Wicho" and an older man that was around sixty-one. Two were students from Puebla. In Sacramento we were sent to Yolo to see what we knew about field work, but since I knew how to drive tractors, and since everyone at the time was fighting the war including mechanics, I stayed. There was a time when one of the tractors was having problems, there were about thirty people working there, I told them that I was a mechanic. I fixed it. But everything was so nice. To tell you the truth, I have never suffered in this country. I got along with my Anglo boss and drove a tractor. My boss did not want me to return to Mexico.
>
> (Interview with Alex Ayala 2002)

Transportation

Transportation was to be adequate and yet it was often not even that. Braceros would simply have to ride in what forms of transportation were provided. The kinds of vehicles used to take braceros from the border to their destination varied from trains, buses, trucks, semi-trucks, to wagons. Getting the Braceros to their final destination seemed far more important than their actual comfort. Don Jesus Saucedo, a bracero I interviewed in Santa Maria, California, describes the condition of the truck used to bring him from the border to the work site:

> I did not know anything about trucks at the time and I wasn't checking. But I knew it was a very uncomfortable truck. We had to sit on the hard wooden floor or remain standing the whole way.
>
> (Interview with Jesus Saucedo 2003)

The lack of decent forms of transportation was very much prevalent. However, once the initial travel from the train or bus from the border was done it was not unusual for them to endure other inadequate transportation. One of the most tragic incidents of braceros killed was at Chualar, California. Ernesto Garlarza's (1977) account in his book, *Tragedy at Chualar,* explained the tragedy of braceros killed crossing a railroad track. Nothing like that was ever discussed with me, thankfully. But I documented several accounts of ill-conceived forms of transportation experienced by braceros.

I did not interview any braceros who experienced or saw any injuries occur to braceros. However, accidents that involved braceros being taken to the camps or fields is well documented (Garlaza, 1964; Garlaza, 1977; Driscoll, 1999). Getting from the camps to the fields was a top priority by growers. Evidence to that fact was the pressure put on braceros to wake up early and get through breakfast as quickly as possible. Don Jose Ramos-Parra describes his early morning routine to get fed before going to the fields:

> **Paul:** You had to wake up very early in the morning?
>
> **Don Jose:** Yes we had to wake up very early in the morning. People would be in line and waiting to get breakfast from 4 or even sometimes at 3 in the morning. For lunch, they would take it all the way where we were working.

To save time, braceros were forced to eat their meals quickly. For example, Don Blas Torino who worked in Woodland, California describes his getting ill because of the unsanitary conditions braceros such as himself experienced:

> **Don Blas:** It was during summer the time that I came down to work in the tomatoes. This time when I came down during June because that's when summer officially starts. It was very hot there. I stayed there from June all the way to December. From there I was sent to San Jose. When I worked in Woodland they would bring us food in cans and they would give you those milk gallons to use. They would force us to eat the food very fast in the field and they didn't care if the people weren't able to wash their hands before they ate the food. You know that the tomatoes are very dirty and because we weren't able to wash our hands I got an infection in my stomach.
>
> **Paul:** How long were you sick for? A month, week, day, or for how long?
>
> **Don Blas:** No, I was sick for a week. I was somehow dehydrated.
>
> **Paul:** Did you talk to a doctor about it?
>
> **Don Blas:** Yes, I told him about it. I said that I was very sick and was dehydrated, so they took me to the doctor. The doctor did some exams on me and told me that I had an infection. He asked what I had eaten. So I told the doctor because he knew how to speak Spanish. I told him that we were forced to eat in the field and that we weren't allowed to wash our hands. So he said that he was going to talk to our boss about it. He gave me medicine for the infection in the stomach and this medication cured the infection.
>
> **Paul:** Did you know any of what happened between the doctor and your boss?
>
> **Don Blas:** After that, they would take all the workers to get their hands washed because a lot of other workers had gotten sick as well from eating the food without washing their hands. In other places people were treated

nicely. You either had the choice to eat your meals quickly or possibly miss the opportunity to work. So the schedule was strict in that regards. Having time to shower and get dressed and then attempt to eat your breakfast before the trip to the fields was quite a task.

Paul: Who did you talk to, to know if you could live there and to know at what time you had to get up for work?

Don Blas: There were some ranchers there, but they were the ones that looked like the contractor or the supervisor of the ranch. He told us that in this place the rules had to be followed. At the ranch at five in the morning everyone has to be up and get ready to work. You have your food ready and yourself ready to work at six o'clock. However if you were not ready by six o'clock you would be left behind and that person will not get to work. In some places there were cafeterias and in other place there weren't any. In the place I ended up called Marysville there weren't any cafeterias, but everyone there was able to cook. But that night the contractor told us that no one was going to urinate anywhere, we don't want any paper on the ground, we don't what any clothes on the ground, everyone that uses dishes must clean his own dishes and whoever doesn't follow the rules will be reported.

For Don Alex Ayala the transportation from the camps to the fields was adequate as he explains his experience. I heard several times that the conditions in Santa Barbara were better than from descriptions of other areas.

Paul: When you worked in Goleta, was transportation a problem?

Don Alex: No, there were big trucks where there was room for everyone. There was even room for water. We did not have a problem at all or have to pay any fees. There was transportation to and from work.

Paul: Was there any seating in the trucks?

Don Alex: Yes, there were benches. We didn't have to sit on the floor.

Paul: How many braceros per truck?

Don Alex: There were around 150 of them, and each would get a pair of plastic boots, and gloves.

Paul: Did you drive any of the trucks?

Don Alex: No, we had drivers. With time those who stayed fixed their paper work and were promoted to managers.

Don Ulbaldo Coronel provides further dismal conditions he endured while traveling to the next work site from the border. Imagine the lack of concern for braceros who were packed into trucks with little in the way of providing even the basic seating accommodations:

Yes, very uncomfortable. On the way to Missouri, since there was no more room in some of the wagons, the rest of the braceros, including myself, had to board a truck with a canvas roof. A bucket was placed in the corner with drinking water and the truck made stops every four hours to use the bathroom. We were treated like animals. It was dark inside the truck and we could not distinguish daylight from darkness. We did not even know where we were going. The trip took a day and a night, and on the way there was a storm that delayed the process and made the road harsh. We also stopped to eat and rest, but I don't understand why we were transported in such conditions.

(Interview with Ulbaldo Coronel, 2002)

Conclusion

The chapter examined the trip which began from the recruiting centers to the border. The trip was more than just a ride. It was their initial experience with how things would continue to be organized—fortunate enough to be selected, but not much luck with the transportation provided. Whether by train or bus, their epic stories would have discouraged most travelers. Ideal conditions were rarely found and having to leave their familiar surroundings for unfamiliar destinations was their frequent experience. The forms of transportation were unfit for human transporting.

Trains did not have comfortable seating. If the trip took more than a day, securing a proper resting place was difficult. At the U.S.-Mexico border, braceros were unloaded and reloaded onto trains, buses, trucks, or other forms of transportation. Depending on the route, braceros were taken to local cities or states requesting them. It appeared little formal planning for even adequate transportation was mandated. Despite the hardships, the trips were endured. Braceros made their way north through sheer willingness to endure these conditions. The inadequate travel accommodations heightened the anxiety of leaving one's home to work abroad. Had there been methods in place for braceros to voice their displeasure perhaps the trip could have been more accommodating. Now, as retired workers, former braceros can look back at those years as just a memory. But those of us less knowledgeable about the sacrifices these men made for themselves and their families can appreciate their stories. These oral histories provide yet another view of the former program decades after its demise. I can appreciate the family members whose children I went to elementary school with and reflect upon the sacrifices made by their parents. For others whom I interviewed, the pattern of hazardous travel conditions remain etched in their memories.

CHAPTER 4

Working in the Fields

Quote from former Mexican Bracero:

I never missed work, not even one day. I never missed one day out of three hundred and sixty five. If I had a hang over I still went to work. I still have my working license and I ask myself why. I can answer my own question because there's no day that I have missed work. I have received letters of praise and congratulations from my boss for not having missed one day of work. I have the best record at work. I wish I can start my life all over again and start working again but this time a bit different.

(Interview with Refugio "Cuco" Gonzalez 2002)

Each of us has to work. Work is a pre-condition. If you want to eat, keep a roof over your head, and support your family, work is essential. In Marxian terms, we've become proletarians. Work becomes our way of fulfilling our obligations. Even teenagers find work at fast food restaurants. For undocumented immigrants, working in a foreign country is a complex experience. Work for undocumented immigrants can be all that they do. Anthropologist Leo Chavez has documented the lives of undocumented immigrants. According to his findings, undocumented immigrants work seven days a week (Chavez, 1993). As the economy continues to polarize low-skill workers, the results are longer hours and less time with their families. Currently, the economic condition of the United States is in dire straits. Unemployment is at an all time high. The privatization of the U.S. government has destabilized the global economy (Klein, 2007).

In a previous chapter (Chapter Two), I explained how braceros were recruited to the United States. The aftermath is today's growing Mexican immigrant community. As a university professor I have the *chore* of having to lecture to young minds. It's a job. I've been teaching well over twenty years and counting. The most I can expect in the way of physical activity is lowering down a screen to present my PowerPoint slides. It's not a bad gig. I'm not always sure it can be defined as a job since I enjoy the work. The *work* I do endure is cleaning my home. Even then, I only do it when I feel the need to find something. My house is by no means a pigsty, but I do have to vacuum and dust. I recall USC professor Pierrette Hondagneu-Sotelo describing her occupation and comparing it to her domestic household chores (Hondagneu-Sotelo, 2007). In short, I have retired elderly parents who *worked*. My mom worked her last nineteen years as a maid cleaning dorms at the university where I spent my post-doctoral year at the Center for Chicano Studies. She got up each day, went to work, and never did I hear her complain. I can't imagine how many dorm rooms she cleaned all those years. Her own home was always spotless. Being the youngest, I was the last one to move out. I don't remember a time when my parents' house was ever as dirty as my own tends to get.

I recall my dad having to work an extra part-time job besides his regular full-time job. At night he would clean office buildings. My uncle (paternal uncle) and the father of one of my best friends also cleaned offices. The memory is still fresh in my mind. My friend's father would drive the same old van (light blue) to downtown Santa Barbara. I could recall vividly seeing his father and (sometimes) his mother in the van going to work. Sometimes if I was lucky I would catch their attention and wave. His parents were both Mexican immigrants. My childhood friend would join his parents after school to help. My close friend went on to U.C.L.A. to earn his bachelor's degree with honors and later attended Stanford University to earn his Ph.D. degree in Chicano literature. His is now an associate professor at Arizona State University. I recall only one time working with my father to clean up an old building that held *Mexican* dances. But it was only to have spending money to buy the latest Doobie Brothers album (yes, I'm that old). I did the work, but it was not going to be my career. I still run into Chicana/o and Latina/o scholars who recall their summers picking in the fields. I don't take my job for granted. If my parents were working today, they could not afford to do what they accomplished: Send their three kids to college and own their own home. In short, the work of low-income workers is heroes work—something to endure, but not reported on the front section of the *New York Times*.

Among the most difficult work to endure is agricultural work. Recently in California a young Mexican woman died of heat dehydration (*Sacramento Bee*, 2007). As the story goes, she was working in Lodi, California and was unable to overcome the lack of water. Workers are to be given ten minute breaks when the heat becomes unbearable. In this case, the water was ten minutes away from the work site. As unfortunate as this death was, there are numerous stories of agricultural workers enduring harsh conditions due to lax labor enforcement. The health and work conditions' of agricultural workers is bleak. This is especially true for the undocumented. One of the problems associated with guest worker programs is that immigrants are at the mercy of employers. The threat of deportation or cancellation of the contract is held over the workers. Unpaid wages or under payment for work can also shortchange guest workers from fulfilling their purpose for migrating.

This chapter examines the field work of braceros. Although several decades removed, former braceros recall their work history rather vividly. Little doubt the work left a memorable impression. The names of former employers or co-workers remain etched in their memories.[1] Work and the time after were crucial. Unable to go back to their families after each day, braceros would make do. If local towns were nearby, weekends were used by braceros to buy goods or send money back home. Entertainment was found at local bars, restaurants, churches, dances, and movie theaters. One view of this experience for braceros is provided by Historian Deborah Cohen. She argues that laboring in the fields and coming home to cook became a form of gender and class transformation. Indeed, she argues that braceros took on gender specific roles. Working all day and then having to come back to the camps and cook their own meals was a new role for them.

> *The same-sex living arrangements contrasted sharply with Mexican domestic ones and affected the ability of braceros to live up to their country's standards of masculinity. In Mexico, domestic arrangements were organized around natal and extended heterosexual family units from which all members derived their economic and social responsibilities and privileges.*
>
> (Cohen, 2008)

Aside from the transitional roles in the camps, the primary role of braceros was as guest workers. According to their contract, braceros were to be assigned specific tasks. From the interviews I conducted, braceros were made to work seven days a week and at tasks not stipulated by the contract. Understandably, employers found the work ethic of braceros to be strong. Braceros would comment on how much their employers would praise their work. Indeed, employers wanted to make sure they rehired the same workers once their contract was expired. However, exploitation was just around the corner. It was clear the interests of growers and not the braceros were the first priority. The stories to follow reveal the difficulties braceros experienced. The chapter also covers their daily life in the camps. The housing conditions were often inadequate. Housing could be make-shift dwellings at best. Protection from the outside elements was not considered.

Braceros and Work

Work was the primary role of braceros. Work was the reason for them to leave family or communities behind. The contract established the work requirements. However, braceros continually found themselves employed at jobs not specified by their contract. Work conditions were far from ideal. Bad weather could deter them from earning enough to send back home.

---

[1] Due to the confidentially of the names recalled in the interviews I used anonymous names to hide the identity of former employers and co-workers braceros mentioned.

Employers were guilty of over-recruiting (Garlarza, 1964). Braceros were unable to work due to an oversupply of workers. The list of problems seemed endless. One of the benefits was the experience of becoming familiar with work sites that would lay the opportunity to return. Indeed, settlement would ensue later. As *pioneer* migrants, the push-pull effects of the Bracero Program would serve to recast their lot. However, eventually it was the social capital earned while in the United States that would help to pave the way for future settlement. In the case of Don Refufio "Cuco" Gonzalez, he details how braceros were able to employ their social networks from the growers who would help them secure their residency.

> *Many rancheros gave letters of recommendation to many braceros. When a lot returned to Mexico they all returned with letters of residency. The company did a good job in giving letters to their workers. When some braceros returned many of them had now become residents and were ready to work. After Johnson Company went out of business we were transferred to another company and that is when many contractors came in and hired many braceros under contracts, picking lemons.*
>
> (Interview with Refugio "Cuco" Gonzalez 2002)

Former braceros also find the opportunity to see one another many years after their bracero migration. The social network of braceros established while in the United States continues to serve them as they see one another to recount their stories or, unfortunately, say their final goodbyes. Don Alex Ayala spoke of a group of braceros who continue to see each another in Santa Barbara:

> *. . . No, we just talk. From the Sacramento group, only four are left. He told me that we should all get together and have dinner. We, Carlos Hernandez and I, often see each other at funerals as well and we talk about coming together once again. We all came from Sacramento, but in Sacramento we were split apart. The rest from my group have died but their group still survives. They are now here in Santa Barbara.*
>
> (Interview with Alex Ayala 2002)

The initial contact of employers and braceros occurred at the border. Border entry points such as El Paso, Texas, or Calexico, California, would provide the first contact. Once at the border, a new set of medical examinations would take place. Looking for diseases or fearing other potential health problems, braceros endured yet another set of medical inspections. Some braceros had an idea where they would go to complete their contracts. Others would not know until they arrived at the work site.

> *The warehouses we were taken to were full but there was enough room for at least two to three thousand people. One would go in and on a chalkboard representatives would write the different assigned counties: San Joaquin, Ventura, Yuma, and different counties in Washington. The ranchers would come in with a microphone and call out the different counties. People, already knowing what county they were assigned, or what grower paid the most, would follow. One would walk in and the translator would inform us of how many braceros the rancher wanted, the hourly*

rate, and the option to work under contract. Those who accepted would have to get in a line. One of the ranchers whom I often saw was called El Zepillo. He only wanted men, no females, to work in San Jose for forty-five days.... This process would take almost the whole day. When our chance came, we would get in line. But there were times when we were not given an option to choose what counties to go to. They would send some people to Yuma, at 85 cents per hour. There would be no other option.

(Interview with Lamberto Garcia 2002)

Now retired and living in Santa Barbara, Don Juventino Cosio spoke of the pay that was to be equal for local workers and braceros. According to Article 15 of the bracero agreement, prevailing wages were expected for braceros and domestic workers. The interview began at a Boot and Western store and then resumed at his home. His grandkids run the store. Now settled, he could recall the dual wages:

Paul: When you worked in Goleta, were all the people braceros?

Don Juventino: No, some were from here.

Paul: Did they pay them the same amount?

Don Juventino: No, they were paid more than us.

Paul: How much?

Don Juventino: I don't know.

Paul: But you do recall that they were paid more than you were.

Don Juventino: Yes.

Paul: Did you say anything?

Don Juventino: No we could not.

Paul: Why not?

Don Juventino: Because the contract was set.

Paul: Did they have a contract?

Don Juventino: Yes, I remember that some people who picked were paid $15 for a big box, others were paid $25.

Paul: In the contract, it says that you guys were supposed to be paid the same.

Don Juventino: But it did not happen.

Paul: You all knew about that?

Don Juventino: Yes, but there was nothing we could do. If you complained, they would tell you that you were going to be sent back.

Paul: They told you that?

Don Juventino: Yes. They told us that we came with that contract and we had to keep it that way.

The combination of lower wages and having to pay for their food would leave the braceros short each week. My interview with Don Lamberto Garcia explains how he was paid differently after the switching from being paid daily to hourly:

> *Picking cotton was very hard because that type of cotton was very tall and the wind would blow it down. We had to pick up the cotton trees and pick the cotton. This took a lot of work but it was little cotton. The first week I picked and others picked about 150 pounds. We would make $4-5 per day and about $30 the whole week. Food was provided for $8.50 per week. From what we earned the whole week, $10 went to food. We would be left with about $20. After the first week, I switched to hourly pay. We were given eight hours and I ended up making $8.50. It was very hard work and the managers were very hard on us.*

(Interview with Lamberto Garcia 2002)

While only supposed to work five days a week, according to the agreement of the contract, braceros were encouraged to work on the weekends. One former bracero lived just around the block from my parents. But it wasn't until I began this project that I became aware of Don Alejandro Gomez. His two sons I knew indirectly. Interviewing Don Alejandro Gomez in his living room after all the previous times I passed his home from school became all too real. Don Alejandro Gomez described how braceros were sought by growers for extra work on the weekend:

Paul: What did you do on your free time, for instance Sundays, when you did not work?

Don Alejandro: Well, a few rancheros from other ranchos came around looking for braceros that wanted to work on Sundays. I was one of those Braceros that preferred to work on Sundays in order to make extra cash.

Don Rafael Carrielo is a former bracero. He explained how braceros were offered extra weekend work, even though that was not part of the contract:

Paul: How many days a week did you work?

Don Rafael: We would work there every day. There weren't any days to rest.

Paul: From what time to what time did you work?

Don Rafael: I would start at 7 am and get out at 5 pm.

Paul: Did you know that you were supposed to get two days off? Did they tell you?

Don Rafael: No, they never said anything about getting days off to rest.

Paul: Did anyone complain about working seven days a week?

Don Rafael: No.

At a bracero meeting in Santa Maria, I was introduced to the organizer of the event. The 10 percent wages that were deducted from braceros was still a big issue and would bring former braceros to community meetings. Don Paulino Pacheco had come as a bracero, and through his own efforts organized meetings. Reaffirming the extra days of work was Don Paulino Pacheco who felt very confined by the working conditions of the camp. Below he describes how difficult the conditions were:

Paul: How many hours did you work as a bracero?

Don Pacheco: We worked from five in the morning to about five or six in the evening. We started early in the morning picking cotton. At noon we would work packing lettuce.

Paul: How many days out of the week?

Don Pacheco: The whole week, sometimes even on Sundays. We worked in a desolate field. The orders were given and you had to obey. You could not go out of town if you were not given permission. There were signs saying what we could and could not do. There were even security guards at the door. It was almost like a prison. You could not go anywhere. We had to ask for permission. We had food in the camp, a small store to buy food as well as a mail office. We were in a prison. One of my friends was telling me that at his camp there were over two thousand braceros. The conditions were the same. It was terrible.

Paul: Did you ever ask for permission to go out of the camp?

Don Pacheco: No you were not given permission even if you asked. You could revolt but if you did you were threatened to be thrown out never to return again. It would stay in your record. Roll was taken and if you were not present you were blacklisted. Some people worked like animals when given a second chance to work again. They did not have any other option. People had to be on the lookout. If you were caught, that was it for you. You had to keep your mouth shut at times.

Paul: When you got sick, did you ever go to the hospital or see a doctor?

Don Pacheco: We had a first aid kit. At some camps, there were a couple of clinics. At times the only thing you would get would be aspirin. I got to see people die due to the heat. The rancheros would just send their bodies back to Mexico. No one ever knew if they sent their pay along with them. People would just collapse at times. All we could do was give them water and put them in the shade. It was impossible to have a nurse right next to you that whole time. These were the conditions.

Other considerations not recognized by growers were the social class of braceros. In the first years of the program, city workers, not peasants from the rural areas, attempted to get contracted. According to Don Amado Carrasco, the first set of workers from Mexico were from the cities and not the stereotypical peasant from rural areas:

A lot of people used to come but they returned after finding out what was happening. The first people that came here to California were not people from the fields. They were not peasants. They were people from the cities, for example Mexico City. Mexico City contracted a lot of people to come and work. . . . There were a lot of people from different economic levels working in the fields. There were people with no education at all, some with a little education, while others had a profession. There was mixture of different class levels. Everyone went with the idea that they were going to someday return again to the United States. I remember when I talked to my wife's father he specifically told me that for 10 cents you were able to cross the border and you were automatically legally in this country and for 25 cents you were an American citizen. That was in the 1900s, but in 1945 and on it was different. I came in 1952.

(Interview with Don Amado Carrasco 2002)

Housing

Providing adequate shelter was not always determined properly. The housing provided was not always under the best conditions. The contract stipulated the housing was to be adequate for braceros. However, below is the actual statement stipulating the sort of housing to be allocated under Article G of the U.S.-Mexico Bracero Agreement:

G. The Mexican workers will be furnished without cost to them with hygienic lodgings, adequate to the physical conditions of the region of a type used by a common laborer of the region and the medical and sanitary services enjoyed also without cost to them will be identical with those furnished to the other agricultural workers in the regions where they may lend their services.

Although written about before, it is worth re-examining the condition regarding housing provided to braceros (Garlarza, 1964; Gamboa, 1987, 2000; Gonzalez, 2007). Many decades afterwards, the memories of the lack of proper housing continued to *haunt* these former guest workers. While interviewing them, their postures changed recalling how difficult it was to endure. Depending upon which state or city they found themselves in, the weather could be extremes of hot or cold. Don Refugio "Cuco" Gonzalez who signed up for the program discusses the living conditions in Arkansas:

I was also in Arkansas picking up cotton for forty-five days as well. I was there for this time and we used to live in an abandoned stable. That's where we were taken. There was nowhere to go and no bathrooms available, nothing. We hooked up hoses for bathrooms and showered with cold water. It was a great sacrifice.

(Interviewed Refugio "Cuco" Gonzalez 2003)

Housing and other facilities remained problematic. Even the smallest thing such as having adequate facilities to clean up after work was not always possible. It was not a random act of one bracero being mistreated when it came to adequate housing, Don Reynaldo provides a picture of the housing in Montana:

Don Reynaldo: Well I was taken to work in Montana and I was there for about three years. We were promised good living conditions, for instance showers, but after getting there we had to shower with cold water at a near-by river.

Paul: Did you know anything about the U.S. before you came to work as a bracero?

Don Reynaldo: No I did not know anything, but I had seen some stuff on TV. When I went to Montana, locals treated us like Indians. It got to the point where we had to protest the inequalities we had to face. There was a time we had to strike in order to have bathrooms with showers. I think our boss believed that we were mentally retarded and would not complain. However, we knew better than that and decided to strike. Braceros from other parts of Mexico, such as pueblos, did not know how to protest or strike and locals took advantage of them.

Another former bracero describes the cold conditions in Arkansas. Don Benjamin Munoz speaks about how cold it was at night:

Paul: Were you provided with housing while working in Arkansas, Nebraska, and Kansas?

Don Benjamin: Well, in Arkansas rooms were divided only by a piece of ply-wood, making it hard to live comfortable and also very cold at night. We were provided with hot charcoals to keep the rooms warm, but it was so cold that water dripping from the faucet turned into icicles. Before going to bed, we often left water in a pot to make coffee in the morning and the water would turn into ice overnight. Arkansas has really cold whether and most of the time it ended up freezing the crop, which was cotton most of the time.

Don Refugio "Cuco" Gonzalez explains the housing conditions located in Texas where facilities for washing their clothes or cooking were not adequately provided:

The conditions were horrible at this place. We did not have any stoves and used a piece of metal to heat up tortillas. I washed my laundry at a nearby stream. There was no order around the place.

(Interview with Refugio "Cuco" Gonzalez 2002)

Housing was sometimes makeshift conditions; indeed, inadequate for human living. Depending on the local weather, the conditions for housing was often poor in colder climate areas. Given the minimal amount of protection from the severe weather, braceros often had to endure the outside weather as best they could.

Paul: When you got off the train, was it during the day or during the night?

Don Rafael: It was during the day around 10 in the morning.

Paul: What happened when you got there?

Don Rafael: We walked to the camps where we were going to stay. It was very close.

Paul: Did they tell you where you were going to sleep?

Don Rafael: In the cargo cars from the trains.

Paul: Did you like where you were staying?

Don Rafael: Sometimes I didn't like it because it got very cold.

Paul: What did you sleep on?

Don Rafael: I slept on the floor.

Paul: Did anyone complain to anybody about how cold it was?

Don Rafael: Yeah, but they wouldn't do anything about it.

Paul: Was there snow outside?

Don Rafael: Yeah, there was a lot of snow.

Paul: Did they complain about it?

Don Rafael: We did complain about it, but they just ignored us.

Further bad housing conditions were reported by Don Lamberto Garcia who spoke about his living conditions while picking cotton in Texas in 1953:

Paul: What type of housing was provided for the braceros?

Don Lamberto: There we slept on racks covered with wire covering. There were no walls and it was dirty. This valley in Texas was very hot and we showered with buckets. We were paid $2.50 for every 100 pounds. But here cotton was much heavier and a lot shorter making it easier to pick. I would pick more than 300 pounds better than before.

Food

Having moved many times over my career as a college professor, I always attempted to find food that reminded me of home. Fresh tortillas or a good tasting carne asada taco always reminded me of being in the Southwest. For braceros, the sacrifice of their favorite foods would sometimes be met if they could cook for themselves. Others would have to rely upon the cuisine available to them. Not all the conditions for eating were provided for the benefit of braceros. Food was brought to the fields and they would have to eat out in the open with the potential of getting sick if the food got mixed in with dirt from the field.

Don Paulino: Yes. From Rancher's Association I was taken to the fields. When I arrived at fields there must have been a thousand braceros working already. I was surprised. We started working early in the morning during the month of July when it got really hot. I would be picking cotton in the morning but during peak heat hour I was taken to clean lettuce. When the sun was going down again we were taken back to the fields. It is a very sad story for the Mexican. Food was bad; it was menudo the whole time.

Paul: With tortillas?

Don Paulino: Yes, with tortillas. For lunch we would sometimes have potato tacos. However, one day a group of braceros decided to revolt because food was bad, water was too hot, toilets were placed far away. We did not even have money for not being paid on time. All we wanted was a change of food, fresh water, and closer toilets. We all revolted. The sheriffs ended up coming along with the Mexican Consul. Instead of helping us, he (Mexican Consul) brought us down. On the other hand, the owner was a man of good heart. He asked us what we wanted and we basically told him to show up to dinner in order for him to see what we ate and what conditions we had to put up with. We also told him what we wanted: good food and fresh water. The boss fired Marcos, the manager, on the spot. Right after that we had the best food, from scrambled eggs to chorizo. It all happened because we revolted. What would have happened if we had not done anything? I could imagine how people feel when they do not have anyone to help them organize.

For Don Agustin Almanza, his impression of the food offered was not acceptable, but he was given little choice on the matter. Working in a Mexican community such as Santa Barbara, California, you would think the food would have been catered toward Mexican workers. But, as my interview revealed, there were little options toward not accepting the food:

Paul: Did you like the food all the time?

Don Agustin: No, not at all the time, but we had no other option.

Paul: How would rate the food?

Don Agustin: It varied every day. Sometimes it was good, and bad at other times. Tortillas were so bad sometimes that they crumbed into pieces in your hands.

Paul: Did you complain to the cooks or to your manager?

Don Agustin: Yes we did. We would tell the guy in charge of the cafeteria.

Paul: Did you think that the cooks did not have much experience cooking?

Don Agustin: Well, food was not the best. We often had refried beans, pork chops grilled in chili; it was mainly food that we were accustomed to eating.

Paul: Did you ever eat out?

Don Agustin: Yes, I did. Since sprayers always were the last ones to arrive, we often missed dinner. It was during those times that I got to eat out. Knowing that we would arrive late, the cook sometimes saved food for us. On Sundays, however, you had to be at the cafeteria on time or else you would miss your meals.

In the following discussion, Don Sacramento Jimenez explained the treatment of cooks toward braceros. Indeed, he details how the food they were promised was not served, but the cooks actually used it for their own purposes:

Paul: Did you like the food?

Don Sacramento: Whether you liked the food or not, you had to eat whatever they gave you. If you did not eat there, you would not eat because we arrived here with no money. The first thing that we do when we get here from Mexico is to send the money to our families. We left them, so we send them money to be sure that they also have something to eat. After a while when you have more money, then you start to make your own food or buy food. In Stockton, we would go eat out on Sundays even though they gave us food, but we were tired of eating the same food.

Paul: Did they give you the same food everyday?

Don Sacramento: No, but they do not cook the food as you would like it to be. They prepare the food differently.

Paul: Did they cook American food all the time? Or do you remember if they also cook carne asada?

Don Sacramento: One time I had a fight with the woman's husband. He asked me how I wanted the eggs and I told him fried, but he gave me scrambled. So I told him I want them fried and he got mad. Then the woman hit me with a scoop. I did not tell her anything. I told the guys that the only thing I had done was to ask for fried eggs and then she hit me, but she did not have a reason to do that. I did not say anything. I told them that I wanted them to be my witnesses and that I was not going to work that day. I went to the bosses' house to let him know what happened. That day I went to their house walking and when I got to their house I told them. In the afternoon they went to the cafeteria. The boss asked them if what I said was truth and they said it was. We had a meeting with the boss and they told the cooks that they should give us whatever we wanted. If we wanted raw eggs, boiled eggs, scrambled eggs, or fried they had to give it to us like that. Then they ask us, what day they gave us meat. They had to give us fish on Fridays and chicken on Sundays. They did not give us meat and they would take that food to their relatives. The boss found out, so from that day on they had to give us better food. The boss told me that if something else happened I should tell him and that he was going to fire her.

Payments, Remittances and Wages

The participation of braceros in the program was due to financial hardship at home. There were very few braceros who I spoke to who did not indicate they were sending money to help support their families back in Mexico. After cashing their checks, sending back money was the next thing they did. Although the money was sent, it did not always provide enough for their families to do well back in Mexico. Remittance among immigrants is a historical consequence of the decision to migrate and is often one of the reasons for the initial migration. Former braceros saw it as their family obligation to help out by providing part of the wages for family members. Was the money sent back enough for families to do well back in Mexico? In most circumstances, the money only helped to get families by for the short-term. Don Alex Ayala explained his reasons for sending money back:

The whole time, I would send money to my mother every fifteen days. In those times we would get paid every ten days. I would get a money order and send it. Whether she needed it or not, I would still send her the money. I always helped her and I have always helped my family. They have never been in need.

(Interview with Alex Ayala 2002)

Investing their money into property was also another reason for money being sent. Interviewing Don Lamberto Garcia of Oxnard, California, there was little doubt his family survival was instrumental on the wages being sent back.

I would leave my wife and kids and come here to work and then send money to Mexico. The money she saved would be used for my next trip. This money was also used to build our house.

(Interview with Lamberto Garcia 2002)

Few braceros I spoke to did not send back money to their families. The money was essential to the needs of family members left behind. Don Agustin Almanza explained the reasons for sending money back to Mexico:

Paul: What was the name of the place called where you went to send money to your family?

Don Agustin: Well, I went to a family working under Jose Aguilar and wife, and the wife was the one that sent the letter along with the money. She would send my family a notice, which included the pickup date and location.

Paul: Do you remember how much you sent?

Don Agustin: I would send about $30 to $40 every fifteen days.

Paul: Why did you send money to your family?

Don Agustin: Well, the money was used to buy the essentials needed around the house such as food and other things. It was also used to buy clothes and whatever necessary for my three kids.

Few interviews did not include how much money was sent back. Nearly every bracero I interviewed spoke about the need to send back money to their families. Don Jesus, now living in Guadalupe, California, explained how much he would send back.

Paul: While you were in Texas, did you ever send money to your family in Mexico?

Don Jesus: Yes, I would send then around $30 to $50. Most of the time it was through money orders.

Paul: Where did you buy your money orders?

Don Jesus: It was a town called Lobo.

---

[2] I had become knowledgeable of the organization headed by Luis Magana. His *Northern California Braceros Association* helped to spearhead the lawsuit. January 5, 2009, was the deadline to submit the required paperwork for the money awarded.

Paul: Did you go all the way there from the rancho?

Don Jesus: Yes, they would take us there.

Occasionally, I would get inquiries about the withheld 10 percent of wages. As part of the initial agreement 10 percent of braceros' wages was to be withheld and deposited in a saving account. For many of the former braceros, the wages were never properly returned to them. My only viable answer to them was to send them toward some of the organizers.[2] Some of the meetings I attended in Salinas, Los Angeles, and Santa Maria discussed the dispute. Below, I asked Don Agustin Almanza about his lost wages:

> **Paul:** Were you informed as to the whereabouts of your deducted money? Were you ever told if it was going to be sent to a Mexican bank where it would somehow become accessible to your family?
>
> **Don Agustin:** I don't remember anything being mentioned about the whereabouts of the money. However, one thing that I do remember being told was the fact that the deducted 10 percent were to be sent to Mexican banks. This is what we were often told but we are not sure whether it was sent or not.

Don Antonio Gomez recalls little about the wages denied. One of the first group of braceros to come to the United States, he came through the program in 1943. He now lives in Santa Barbara with his wife who he met while working as a bracero.

> *After the war when people were still coming, but I don't know if they took away the 10 percent that they took from us, but when I came they did tell us because it was an agreement with the government.*
>
> (Interview with Antonio Gomez 2002)

Don Paulino Pacheco, who I mentioned earlier, spoke of his attempts to figure out where the 10 percent deducted from wages went. Little information was provided to former braceros about where the money had disappeared. There still appears to be a disagreement whether the money ever made it to Mexico, or if it did, was it fraudulently stolen.

> **Paul:** While you were working how were you paid?
>
> **Don Paulino:** Some only paid you with check.
>
> **Paul:** Were you ever given the share of the money that was sent to Mexico? Was money taken away from your check?
>
> **Don Paulino:** Ten percent was always taken away. That 10 percent was taken out automatically when you received your check. My brother, the one that lives in Washington and who worked in the diary company, asked why the 10 percent was taken away. He was told that the Mexican government wanted that money. A lot of braceros did not know that this percent was taken away from their pay. It was the *Convenio Bracero Mexico Americano* that took the percentage away. The question now is who and where the money is.
>
> **Paul:** Did you ever ask your wife if she ever got the money?
>
> **Don Paulino:** No.

Paul: Did you ever ask your boss?

Don Paulino: No, I never did. We all believed we had a savings account and could retrieve the money when we returned to Mexico. Time passed and no one ever claimed the money while working.

Paul: Where would you cash your check?

Don Paulino: At the local store. Like I told you we had a store at the camp.

Conclusion

This chapter examined the work and labor camp experience of braceros. Working in the fields and daily life in the labor camps proved to be problematic. Balancing work and the time to eat a meal similar to what they were used to became another issue of contention. Braceros felt the pressure to be at work on time and rising early to get to breakfast was a timely experience. If you were late for breakfast, nothing was served after the trucks left for the fields. In short, rising as early as four in the morning to wash up and then make breakfast on time was part of their daily regime. Routinely the meals were the same. And if there were attempts to provide meals similar to the ones back in Mexico, it was often second rate. I suppose if one is brought in as an immigrant guest worker, there is not the expectation that meals would be catered to you. Yet, in some cases these workers were coming to traditional Mexican communities. Others were working in states or cities where there was no Mexican community. Cities in the Midwest and Southwest states were least likely to have Mexican food.

Sacrifices tended to be the norm for braceros. Leaving family behind and then experiencing harsh working conditions and inadequate camp life became all too common. On top of that, the cultural divide between braceros and locals further complicated their experience. As some Mexican braceros suggested, they were identified by their foods. Indeed, as Deborah Cohen's study suggested braceros were men, but also identified by the food they ate.

> *The differences between Mexico and the U.S. to which braceros referred, ones marked by new sleeping arrangements and kinds of music, extended to routines around eating and food eaten. When I spoke with these men accustomed to a diet of tortillas and beans, they halfheartedly complained about the food and the "lack of tortillas.*

> (Cohen, 2006)

Years after their initial migration, I was routinely surprised how much these former guest workers remembered. Working and living conditions were just exactly what other studies had revealed. But many decades removed, their stories were still vividly embedded. Hoping for the best, they got less in return than they expected by signing up for the program.

CHAPTER 5

Braceros and Settlement in the United States

My name is Francisco Mejica, I live in Chico, California. I am 64 years old and I am from Michoacan, Mexico. . . . When my mom was alive I would go visit her. I would go to San Antonio, Michoacán. I still have family there like my brother and nephew. I also have family here in Chico. Like my nephews and cousins, some live here in Chico and some in Orland. I like it here because there is work here, my family is here and a lot of trees as well. I want to go back to Mexico, but then I want to stay here. I would go to Mexico for like three months, but I don't know about staying there.

Quote from former barcero who is now settled.

When I think back to my last few days of elementary school, the one day that I remember most was the parent-teacher conference. By all measures I was a restless kid. I did only what was necessary to complete my school work. Finishing eighth grade, all students met with our teacher and parents. It was the exit interview before going on. It was a day I would never forget. My teacher informed my parents on that day that I would drop out of high school. To this day, my mom still recounts that memory. My parochial school was by no means the best in Santa Barbara. Most of my classmates were two years behind the reading standards. The school was located in the Chicano/Mexican barrio of the eastside of Santa Barbara. The residents of that portion of the community were either first generation Mexican immigrants or two generations removed from Mexico. It was a working class section of the community. I recall just around the block from the school a family operated *panadería* (Mexican bakery). When I had extra money, I would treat myself to *pan dulce* (sweet bread). My classmate's father, a Mexican immigrant, ran the store. My former classmate now runs her own *panadería* on the west side of Santa Barbara. Admittedly, attending Our Lady of Guadalupe was the best thing I did. As classmates, we became life-time friends. However, as we got older there were fewer reunions or opportunities to see one another.

The distance from my childhood to where I am now is still relevant. Now middle-aged, I continue to service a new generation of college students who make teaching quite demanding. When I began teaching, there were no cell phones or iPods. Now there are wireless connections in classrooms. I'm concerned that students are updating their facebook accounts on their laptops while I'm lecturing. I was a mere twenty-five years old when I first began college teaching. After completing my master's degree in sociology from the University of Notre Dame, I had the opportunity to teach my first Chicano Studies history course at the community college in Santa Barbara. My former professor remembered me and gave me my first break. Married and with my first child recently being born, I had no time to reflect upon my two years at Notre Dame and what I had just accomplished. No sir, it was taking care of my son during the day. Once my wife (now ex-wife) got home from work, I would use the rest of the evening to prep for my college class. I was a young professor. I was only about four or five years older than some of the students I was teaching. I was both excited and scared. It was so long ago that when I would show a film I used 16 millimeter projectors. One memorable moment was starting a film and witnessing it fly off the front of the projector. Trying to ward off further disasters, I attempted to catch the thundering film but to no avail. The film was all wrapped up against itself and I don't recall if it could be fixed or repaired back to its original state. Thankfully, college professors can use DVDs today.

As a college professor I speak to my students about what they can expect to see regarding the racial make-up of the United States. My students seem to be puzzled that I am looking ahead to when they are middle aged. There are over 300 million Americans (as of this writing) identified by the U.S. census. By 2050, the United States will be 400 million people. When the United States reached the 300 million mark in November of 2007, the occasion was marked by the logical projection that a Latino baby was the 300th American born on that day. Indeed, other signs that the U.S. is darkening racially is provided by the rise in Latino surnames. For the first time, the surnames of Latinos are now competing with Anglo surnames. Indeed, among the top ten surnames listed by the census, Garcia and Rodriguez had reached the top ten. Here is what a *New York Times* article had to say:

> *Smith remains the most common surname in the United States, according to a new analysis released yesterday by the Census Bureau. But for the first time, two Hispanic surnames—Garcia and Rodriguez—are among the top ten most common in the nation, and Martinez nearly edged out Wilson for tenth place.*
>
> (*New York Times*, 2007)

This chapter examines the settlement of Mexican braceros. The analysis of settlement is both a personal and academic examination. Looking back, I realize that I was directly and indirectly affected by the former U.S.-Mexico Bracero Program. Indeed, there is no disconnecting my childhood to my adulthood. The social network described by the social capital theory perspective is relevant. Although my father wasn't a bracero, he worked alongside them and served as an interpreter. My uncle used to drive the company trucks that would take braceros to the fields each day. I went to elementary school with children of braceros. I continue to meet and interview braceros through my students and colleagues. I even worked with a former bracero at the parking lot when I worked for the city of Santa Barbara while attending the local community college.

The program's legacy is a personal story for me as well as an academic study. The bridge between the two is blurred by the fact that I was directly involved with the program. Indeed, during my childhood I lived on a ranch where braceros worked. And I continue to be related to the program through my research from this project. In many ways this examination of the settlement of former Mexican braceros is also my story. The stories to follow describe how settlement occurs. The further I probed with the interviews I conducted, the more I saw the direct relationship I had with the program. And as a scholar I also saw how other families were directly connected to the program. In short, this chapter examines how the program was the basis for Chicano and Mexican families to establish the ties that would lead to settlement.

My earlier discussion of social theory and migration helps to place the examination of settlement. As the reader recalls, the social capital embedded by braceros as temporary workers served them later, allowing for possible settlement. Continued migration either during the program or after their bracero migration established the social network necessary for continued migration. Eventually, the prior migration would help to lower the cost of migration. Indeed, as Massey, Durand and Malone (2002) point out when they state the following:

> Migrant networks are an important source of social capital for people contemplating a move abroad. They are a set of interpersonal ties that connect migrants, former migrants, and nonmigrants at places of origin and destination through reciprocal ties of kinship, friendship, and shared community origin. They increase the likelihood of international migration movement because they lower the costs and risks of movement and increase the expected net returns to migration.

Although there are braceros who are now living their remaining lives in Mexico, the braceros who remain in the United States are experiencing their elderly years differently. These former guest workers served as the first step toward an American story. Immigrants have come to the United States for various reasons: as war refugees, as indentured servants, and to escape poverty. Mexican braceros came as recruited labor. Now, as permanent settlers, their stories are relative to the current discourse on Mexican immigration. The stories that follow are an attempt to place their lives within a past and current content. Indeed, the time that has passed since their initial migration remains relative toward explaining their current status. When I write these stories into the following narrative I feel myself as part of the story as well as being able to explain just how relative the guest workers become a part of the United States.

New Era in America

Current population change is leading to the *darkening* of the racial landscape in America. The bulk of racial change is from Asian and Latin American immigrants. Throughout the United States and Western Europe, there is decline in the white population. This is leading to increasing population shortages. Since 1965, changes to the immigration laws favor family or kinship sponsorship. Economic development in Latin America and Asia are also fueling potential migration. Unable to find economic opportunities in their own countries, immigrants and their families are using migration as the means to support themselves (Portes and Rumbaut, 2006; Hondagnue-Sotelo, 2007). Mexican immigrants, both documented and undocumented, continue to find avenues to enter. To the chagrin of nativists who fear a rebirth of a Mexican state or *La Reconquista*, anti-Mexican hate crimes are rising (Buchanan, 2002; Chavez, 2008). A recent report of hate crimes against Latinos by the Southern Poverty Law Center confirms increased hate crimes (Potok, 2008). Conservatives such as Rush Limbaugh continue to blame all of our societal ills on Mexican immigration. Indeed, during the previous century Mexicans were blamed for the Great Depression, loss of manufacturing jobs, the decline of Western Civilization, and even the recent swine flu outbreak was blamed on Mexican immigration (Schlesinger, 1998; Buchanan, 2002; Hanson, 2003).

It would seem a country composed of immigrants since its inception would have a positive attitude toward them (Zinn, 2003; Hondagnue-Sotelo, 2001; Portes and Rumbuat, 2006). But the story repeated too numerous to be accounted for this book, rejects immigrants who desire to contribute to the country (Takaki, 1989; Light, 2004; Zuniga and Hernandez-Leon, 2006). In Escondido, California, for example, city officials have attempted to punish undocumented immigrants. At the core of the Escondido stand off are the costs to educate their children or provide for social services. Check points by local police remind the Mexican American and Mexican community of the racial profiling they endure. Chapter One mentioned the previous attempts to directly punish immigrant children for the decisions that their parents made. Court cases usually end with the constitutional rights of undocumented immigrants defended (Flores, 1982).

U.S. cities that have gone the similar route toward punishing immigrants often experience financial economic downturns. The city of Hazelton, Pennsylvania adopted an anti-immigrant stance. After driving most of the undocumented immigrants from Hazelton, city officials found the city struggling to meet its financial obligations. Immigrants with their strong work ethic can fuel the resurgence of local economies as they begin to invest money into the cities' economies. Besides serving the immigrant population, native-born Americans begin to benefit. Economic resurgence of communities occurs as immigrants become the economic stimulus of stagnant economies. Although, immigrants will first service their own communities, over time the extension of services extends to non-immigrants. In short, immigrants will provide additional jobs that are created or maintained when immigrants begin to find their economic niche in local economies.

For whatever costs immigrants entail upon a city, the return in the start of new businesses exceeds their integration. Long-term gains can also occur from using public money to educate the children of immigrants. Investing in the education of children from immigrant families tends to be in the best interest for America. It appears we haven't quite learned that lesson. The current *Dream Act* attempts to allow access to education for students whose parents brought them over without the legal documents.

We remain a country that continues to view immigrants to America as invaders or hordes on the verge of overrunning the traditions which are gradually becoming an American way of life. Indeed, we continue to attack immigrants who often are behind the revigoratioring of various sectors of the American economy (Portes, 1994; Light, 1972; Bonacich, 1973). Previous groups who have come to the United States and experienced the backlash of simply being immigrants looking for opportunities have been the Chinese, Japanese, Irish, Italians, Germans, Filipinos. Koreans, East Indians, and others. In short, the story of Mexican braceros likely living their final years in the United States brings the story of immigrant settlement full circle. The initial supporters of the U.S.-Mexico Bracero Program did not expect to see former braceros as settlers in the United States, but expected them to remain temporary workers. However, the legacy has been that braceros, and now their families, are permanently tied to the United States.

One criticism of guest worker programs is the likelihood of permanent settlement (Reubens, 1986; Castles, 1986). Guest worker programs provide the initial incentive toward migrants finding the opportunities open to them after spending significant time in the host country (Martin, 2002). One could possibly argue that settlement of braceros began before they finished their contracts. Once in the United States, Mexican braceros could see how life in the United States offered economic opportunities not possible in Mexico. In addition, employers in the United States also saw the strong work ethic among braceros. Not only did employers encourage braceros to renew their contracts, but many employers went out of their way to keep the same workers employed at their ranches after their contracts had expired. Personal relationships between braceros and their employers occurred during the programs' existence. As one former bracero describes his relationship with his employer, it helps to explain how permanent settlement was a two-way street for braceros and their employers:

> When the Bracero Program was over, my boss told me that I had to return to Mexico, however, he told me that if I wanted to stay he would help me in getting my residency. I gave him all the paperwork he needed and he was able to get my residency. He made (wrote) a letter for me and sent it to the Consulate.
> (Interview with Benjamin Munoz on 2003)

As I pointed out earlier in the theoretical section of the book, once an immigrant makes multiple trips back and forth a social network is created. Each migrating experience becomes somewhat easier and less costly. The social capital that migrants build upon is called upon repeatedly as the knowledge of where to cross or where they are likely to return to become valuable resources. For braceros now permanently settled in the United States this cannot be overstated. Upon crossing the border either at El Paso, Tijuana, Nogales, or any other entry point, braceros became acquainted with persons and places that would serve them later.

Paul: How long were you here as a bracero?

Don Ramon: 1960, '61, '62, '63, it was about four years, but I wasn't here the entire four years. The first year I only came for three months in 1960.

Paul: Where?

Don Ramon: To the Imperial Valley. I was there from April until July of that year. The contract ended and they told us there wasn't much work, that if we wanted to stay we could wait here until there was work or if we wanted to we could go back to Mexico. So I left to Mexico. It is then that they gave me this paper. This paper meant that when I wanted to come back to work I could just present this and they would know that I had already been here, that I already knew the area and that they already knew me as well.

Repeated contracts signed by braceros also gave them further knowledge of the economic benefits of returning or staying over once their contract ended. Some braceros also saw their time in the United States as too problematic. Either they were too lonely to stay and opted out of their contract, or they began to consider bringing their families to the United States. It's hard to estimate just how many chose either option. But it was clear from the interviews conducted that former braceros were seeking what was best for them and their families. Don Rafael Carrielio who came in December of 1942 to work in Illinois later returned to the United States, but not until 1969. His contract experience as a bracero was not enough to re-sign another contract. He came back because he had family in the United States.

Paul: What year did you return to the United States?

Don Rafael: In 1969.

Paul: Where did you go to work?

Don Rafael: I came to California to work.

Paul: Did your bracero experience help you decide to come back to the United States?

Don Rafael: No it wasn't about my experience as a bracero; it was about my family.

Employers and Braceros

What became a continuous theme found among the braceros I interviewed for this book was their eventual settlement in the United States. How they were able to secure their settlement was a result of the information they were able to secure during their time as immigrant guest workers. Besides the economic contributions braceros were able to provide to employers, braceros were viewed as dependable or reliable workers. Employers' enthusiasm for the work ethic braceros brought to their work sites added to their settlement (Schmitter-Hessler, 2007; Gamboa, 2000). Despite the requirement of braceros to return to Mexico after completing their contracts, braceros were sometimes already thinking about how they could continue to work in the United States. As my conversation with Don Alex Ayala revealed, he became reluctant to return to Mexico due to the lack of work:

Paul: When you were working here did you ever think of returning to Mexico?

Don Alex: Well, at first I wanted to return to Mexico. Between the first three months I wanted to return. But I then saw that I was making money and decided to stay for a few more months. Two years before getting married I would constantly visit Mexico. I no longer had a job in Mexico and it was and still is hard to get a job in Mexico. At that time I hadn't started saving up money and there was no way I could stay. I, on the other hand, returned to keep working. The employer and employee relationship is not a new experience for immigrants.

The signing of the contract was to be the deal that ensured braceros would be temporary workers. Yet, all too often the contract was the stepping stone for braceros to gain further knowledge regarding their opportunities of possibilities in the United States. As one former bracero recalls, his decision to stay beyond his contract became stronger as he reached the border. At the border, contracts were able to be renewed without having to go back into Mexico. Don Juventino describes how he was given the opportunity to renew his contract:

> *They would take us to a corral in El Centro (He means Calexico, California). Over there they would tell us that our contracts were over and give you a document that would help you in case they want to contract more people. You could come again and work, just if you wanted, you were not going to be forced.*
>
> (Interview with Juventino Cosio on 2002)

The employers often served as go betweens. If an employer wanted to ensure access to the same worker, he would go out of his way to help secure another contract or legalize their residency status. Employers would attempt to either rehire braceros or go out of their way to legalize their status. The relationship between bracero and employer, although not always harmonious given the abuses recorded, did lead to being able to work toward continued employment. As my interview with Don Jose Ramos-Parras of Ojai, California revealed, there were mixed feelings about choosing which country offered the best opportunities:

> *Sometimes I don't know which place is better because I have half my family here and the other half in Mexico. Both places are good, but the United States just gives you a chance to come here and work. If it was for that people would come and bother this place.*
>
> (Interview with Jose Parra-Ramos on 2005)

The relationship between employers and workers cannot be understated. Indeed, many employers took advantage of braceros. There is no disputing that, and it has been well documented (Garlarza, 1964; Driscoll, 1999; Schmitter-Hessler, 2007). Occasionally, growers would step in and help to secure the residency of braceros. Growers would get them to stay over past their contract deadline. Don Adolfo was among those as he spoke to me about working in Texas. He had come to the United States to help support his family. He had worked on his family's ranch and had experience picking cotton. Don Adolfo had skills beyond simply working in the fields. Below, he recalls how his employer arranged to get him to legalize his status to get him to stay beyond his contract:

The reason I came was because I had to help my family. I was the oldest. I worked in Mexico but it was not sufficient. The opportunity came for me to go to Texas, I was lucky and I had good bosses. I had to pick lemons, and then I got to be a weightier. I told the boss that I was a skilled mechanic and one time a truck broke and I fixed it. My job became easier. I was contracted then, later I was contracted again. My boss asked for me to contract again. I told the boss that I would come back and work if he helped me with immigration status. He said yes, and in less then forty-five days I had an appointment. I got my green card, and I turned in the items to work again.

(Interview with Adolfo Perez on 2002).

Braceros and Their Wives

Braceros also could be seen meeting Mexican American women who they would marry and then would find ways to secure their permanent settlement with their new brides. Establishing new relationships abroad is not uncommon. From the perspective of former braceros, the idea of not being able to come into contact with the Mexican (American) community would seem unlikely. Many braceros came into communities where other Mexican (Americans) had already settled decades before, after years of prior migration, especially in the early years of the program's existence. My conversation with Don Juventino Cosio and his wife offered insight into their decision to stay in the United States. Here is what Don Juventino and his wife had to say about how they got their legal papers:

> **Don Juventino:** They might also say that we are *un emigrado*, that is like telling you that you are American, because they think that because we immigrated to the United States we are from here. The first time I went back, I had problems with the language because there are different words for one thing, so I would get confused because people would use words that I used but in a different context. I did not know the different meanings for a word because I came here when I was young. Here, we use different words in Spanish and over there they use others.

> **Paul:** Do you remember how many times you went back to Mexico?

> **Don Juventino:** I would go every year.

> **Paul:** Still?

> **Don Juventino:** Not anymore. I do not even have relatives over there. All the family came here. My wife has only two brothers over there.

> **Paul:** Do you still talk to your family in Mexico?

> **Antonia:** My mom is over there.

> **Paul:** Do you write to her?

> **Antonia:** I call her.

> **Paul:** Are you planning on going back?

Antonia: He is sick, we can't go.

Paul: But if he were not sick, would you go there?

Antonia: Just to visit, not to live.

Paul: Is it really important?

Antonia: No, but I like to go and eat over there.

Paul: Is the food better over there?

Antonia: We are used to that food.

Paul: Would you go to Mexico even if you did not have family there?

Don Juventino: I would not.

Paul: It is not important to you anymore?

Don Juventino: I don't have my mother. I only have a nephew.

Braceros would tell me stories of meeting women from the towns where they were contracted. Don Agustin Almanza, who came early in the program, recalls how he met his wife while working in Santa Barbara, California. He spoke of that time very fondly. By the time of my interview, his wife had already passed away. I was able to learn more about their family from his daughters who now take care of him.

> *I used to work with her brother Isidro and when we did not work on weekends he used to invite me to his house. My wife used to live a few houses away and she used to come and see us. This is how I started to know her and later started dating her. At the time, she was going through a divorce and later decided to marry me in 1946. In 1947 I decided to go back to Mexico to apply for my residency. I had to go to San Luis Potosi, where one of my uncles lived, and he knew the area. He took me to the American Consul and that same day I received my residency. I took with me what they required and in no time I was ready to come to the U.S. as a resident.*

(Interview with Agustin Almanza on 2002)

Braceros and Their Children

If there is a bigger story to tell about the settlement of braceros, it is the securing of a better life for the children of braceros. When I went into the homes of braceros to speak to them about their experiences as braceros, there were few occasions when I did not hear about their children. The children of braceros were mostly grown adults now, finding their way in the United States both personally and professionally. For all the rhetoric of the negative consequences of immigrant settlement, the positive aspects are the children of former braceros. Time and time again, the success of former bracero children was helped by their establishing roots in the United States. I want to use this section to give the accounts of how some of the braceros speak of their children as Americans or immigrant children living the American dream. Don Jose Ramos-Parras speaks of his children in the United States and his reasons for thinking about possibly staying in the United States:

> **Don Jose:** Sometimes I don't know which place is better because I have half my family here and the other half in Mexico. Both places are good, but the United States just gives you a chance to come here and work. If it was for that people would come and bother this place.
>
> **Paul:** Why has this country been good to you?
>
> **Don Jose:** This country has been good to me because it gives me the opportunity to work and make money to help my family have a better life, because in Mexico you really can't sustain a family.

Other braceros were more forthright with their decision to stay permanently. In my interview with Don Sacramento Jimenez of Santa Barbara, he spoke of the advantages or opportunities that the United States offered. He spoke of his decision to remain in the United States. His wife and children were the main reasons for staying:

> **Paul:** Are you planning on going back to Mexico?
>
> **Don Sacramento:** Right now?
>
> **Paul:** Do you go for vacations?
>
> **Don Sacramento:** I do go on vacations, but right now I am living here. I go to Mexico every year, at the end of the year.
>
> **Paul:** Why?
>
> **Don Sacramento:** Because I have my mother over there and my family, my brother.
>
> **Paul:** So you are the only one living here and your wife?
>
> **Don Sacramento:** I have all of my family here. All of my children are here. In Mexico I have my brother, my two sisters, my mom. I have people over there that I can go and visit. So every year I go. Whenever I can, I send her money.
>
> **Paul:** Still?
>
> **Don Sacramento:** Yeah, all of my siblings do it too. We each send her a few dollars.
>
> **Paul:** Why don't you bring her over here?
>
> **Don Sacramento:** She does not want to come here. She won't come over here. That's why I go there every year. The last time I went, I was there for two months. At work they gave me vacations for a month, but I told them that I needed more time to be with her because she is really old. I am still working, but only four days.

Having children to raise also helps to determine where braceros would eventually settle. Don Antonio Gomez and his wife had to make the decision where they would settle. In their case, it meant selling property in Mexico and leaving behind anything that would further tie them.

Mrs. Antonio Gomez (wife of Don Antonio Gomez) explains how the decision was made to remain rather than retire in Mexico:

> **Paul:** Is he still a citizen of Mexico?
>
> **Mrs. Antonio Gomez:** He is still a citizen. He never wanted to drop his citizenship, because his plan was to go back to Mexico after he retired and he bought property over there. I did not want to go back over there. I spent four years over there. After he retired I told him we would spend some time over there, but he really wanted to live over there and after a while he said, "Well our kids are over there, what are we going to do over here." I told him, "That's what I said, so if something happens to us over here, the kids can't come to claim nothing because they don't know the laws, the language, they don't know how to read." He decided to sell the land that we had and we just settled down.

Don Alejandro Gomez's decision to remain in the United States was quite simple. Having his children in the United States and growing up from the time they were born enabled him to quickly decide to remain. He was now well into his eighties and retired.

> **Paul:** Since you married a person born here in the U.S., was it easier for you to adopt to stay here?
>
> **Don Alejandro:** Yes, I believe this made the process easier even though I had grown up in Mexico. As a matter of fact, I spent the last part of my youthful years and my adulthood here in the U.S. All my family is here now and I don't see a reason for me to return to Mexico.

Legal Status

Many braceros saw the advantage of staying over after completing their contracts. Enough of them knew that getting their legal papers in order would help them to remain in the United States. The legacy of the program would ensure that each generation of migrants would settle after either returning to Mexico or simply staying over illegally until the papers were in order. In the case of Don Ramon Martinez, he found legal help by getting a lawyer to legalize his status:

> *The lawyer who was fixing everything for me charged me $50 for everything. So I went ahead and wanted to fix everything to get my papers. The others that had gone with me did have the money, but they felt that $50 was way too much money. It was a lot of money by the way we earned it, but this money was going to go toward something good. Spending money for a good cause was not a lot of money. I then had to leave, but I took the lawyer's address and that of someone who lived in Santa Paula, a Mexican who had a market and we all knew him by "El Chino." I never knew his real name. He knew us because we would buy things there at his market. He knew us for awhile, so when the lawyer came, I took him to the market to give him proof that I had given the lawyer $50. I used "El Chino" as a witness.*

And the lawyer gave me a receipt. So when I left to Mexico in August of 1963 I started to look for the papers in Mexico that were required for the legal documentation to enter the U.S. Nothing was very difficult then because I had money. You had to go to the department of justice to get a letter of recommendation, which they check you for criminal activity and you have to list those people who know you, you have to state your marital status, and having money made it fairly effortless.

(Interview with Ramon Martinez in 2003)

Others used whatever methods available to stay over rather than go back. Having family members already in the United States enabled braceros to simply skip going back. In the case of Don Francisco Ordaz, he simply left after his contract was over and headed to where he had extended family. I taught his grandson, who is legalized and now settled here, in one of my Chicano Studies courses.

> **Paul:** What happened after the time you were there? Did you go back to Mexico?
>
> **Don Francisco:** I called my uncle and told him I wanted to go to Orland. I had family here and he sent someone to get me in like two days. I told him I would be dressed in a certain way and what the guy would be wearing that was picking me up. I saw him and went to Orland. I was all wet when I got here.
>
> **Paul:** Did anyone tell you that you had to go back to Mexico?
>
> **Don Francisco:** Everything was good here and there was no immigration. I was supposed to go straight to Mexico, but I wanted to make more money so I stayed with my uncle. I found someone that helped me get my papers.

Don Salvador Munoz, who has now settled, recalls what he did to return to the United States. Like so many of his fellow countrymen from Zacatecas who came from Mexico, he only has a few family members who remain in Mexico:

> **Paul:** Did want to come again to the U.S.?
>
> **Don Salvador:** Yes. I came again but this time I went to Tijuana to get my passport. I have been here in this country for forty years already. There was a period when I did not go back to Mexico for about twenty years. All the males of my age are all here in the U.S. Out of all the times that I have returned to Mexico, I have not found one person that I know that is living there. All of them have families here now and a lot are grandparents. Out of eleven in my family, only three are left in Mexico. This is visible in every house in Zacatecas.
>
> (Interview with Salvador Munoz on 2003)

Speaking to Don Francisco Mejica, who I met through one of my online students, I asked him about his experience while working in Chico, California. He contracted twice and after going back to Mexico after his second contract was over he came back to the United States through family he had in Los Angeles. His wife had a sister in Los Angeles who helped them cross from Tijuana. Having extended family in Chico, he was able to move his family from Los Angeles to Chico where he and his wife began working in agricultural work. He mentioned that having family here led him to legalize his status after coming back the United States as an undocumented immigrant following his bracero migration.

Paul: Were there a lot of Mexicans here?

Don Francisco: There weren't that many Mexicans. When I came I had a sister here, she had her family here already. Then we came here. After seven years we got papers here. My daughter is from Chico.

Paul: Did you go back to Mexico?

Don Francisco: For a couple of days to see my brothers. When my mom was alive I would go visit her. I would go to San Antonio, Michoacán. I still have family there like my brother and nephew. I also have family here in Chico. Like my nephews and cousins, some live here in Chico and some in Orland. I like it here because there is work here, my family here, and a lot of trees as well. I want to go back to Mexico, but then I want to stay here. I would go to Mexico for like three months, but I don't know about staying there.

Conclusion

This chapter examined the settlement of braceros. Labeled a temporary guest worker program, it never lived up to its temporary status. Indeed, as others have documented, guest worker programs feed into long-term consequences. The U.S-Mexico Bracero Program was no different. Its legacy remains ingrained. The children and the grandchildren of braceros are now Americans. They redefine the term American. For some critics, the growing presence of Mexicans in the United States is seen as a threat. Continued Mexican immigration during this current century will redefine the racial landscape. The evolving of a Protestant Anglo-Saxon nation to one that is becoming more diverse each year is challenging hardliners. Yet, the legacy of Mexican immigration is indebted to the former program.

The social capital that enabled former braceros to remain or return to the United States is fueling the current generation of Mexican immigration. The social network has been in place for many decades, beginning with the first wave of braceros in 1942 entering through the program, until 1964. Now that legacy is instilled in the migration patterns of current Mexican immigrants. Indeed, the legacy of the former Bracero Program continues to influence today's migrants. It's a legacy that continues to feed other migrants from Mexico in the hope that their lives will be better. Early signs of the current economic downturn suggest that fewer migrants are crossing or going back to Mexico (Hopfensperger, 2009). Should the economy of the United States bounce back, the likely scenario is a rise in the number of Mexican immigrants to the United States rather than take their chances back in Mexico.

CHAPTER 6

Conclusion

Therefore, I support a temporary worker program that would create a legal path for foreign workers to enter our country in an orderly way, for a limited period of time. This program would match willing foreign workers with willing American employers for jobs Americans are not doing. Every worker who applies for the program would be required to pass criminal background checks. And temporary workers must return to their home country at the conclusion of their stay. A temporary worker program would meet the needs of our economy, and it would give honest immigrants a way to provide for their families while respecting the law. A temporary worker program would reduce the appeal of human smugglers and make it less likely that people would risk their lives to cross the border. It would ease the financial burden on state and local governments, by replacing illegal workers with lawful taxpayers. And above all, a temporary worker program would add to our security by making certain we know who is in our country and why they are here.

(President George W. Bush, 2007 State of the Union Speech)

Back in those days we didn't think of anything only adventures. None of us were campesinos. We came looking for adventures. We ended up settling here and did not see a point in returning. Like I told you before, within three months I wanted to return as well, then time passed and we stayed. It's been sixty years and I haven't returned.

(Interview with Alex Ayala 2003)

From the beginning, this book evolved from a family conversation. Had I known about my family's ties to the U.S-Mexico Bracero Program, it would have shortened my graduate school years. My dissertation could have covered this topic.[1] I suspect that, similar to the braceros I interviewed, my parents felt their personal history was not important. I was also able to learn about the involvement of other Chicano and Mexican families with the program. It also brought back a host of childhood memories—memories I thought forgotten. For example, I recall each year racing my (male) schoolmates to see who was the fastest. It was a big deal. We had a bond that extended beyond school. Beginning as first graders, each year we *renewed* our friendships. For eight years we were extended brothers. Occasionally we got new members. Eventually, the new member would be part of the group. Our Catholic parochial school was among the most ethnically diverse. Diversity was limited to Mexican Americans, Mexicans, and sprinkled in-between Anglo kids, and the occasional African American or Asian student. We had nicknames based upon our physical or personality differences. Even the girls from our peer group had been *tagged* appropriately. When you truly wanted to get someone's attention, all you had to do was evoke their nickname.

Of course, as kids, we didn't think much about our family's history. We were mainly concerned about important things, the fastest among us. To determine who was the fastest, we would line up at the open-air cafeteria and begin racing. I think in all the eight years I attended Our Lady of Guadalupe I was only once the fastest. As we grew older, someone new would reign as the running champ. It was a big status-evoking rite of passage. I recall toward the end of my tenure when the least likely of the group became the fastest. He had grown over the summer and his lanky legs propelled him to win the title. My running specialty was playing freeze tag. I would use the building circular poles as a mechanism to reverse my running direction in a split second. Even the nuns witnessing me were impressed. Probably our highest priority was avoiding punishment by the nuns. Indeed, very hard to do as you can imagine.

On rare occasions now I "bump" into my former schoolmates. I now realize how *different* their family life was to mine. My parents spoke to me and my siblings mostly in English. Growing up my mom learned from her teachers that speaking Spanish was punishable. Her burritos from home were made fun of. Now K-12 kids reject bologna sandwiches in favor of a diverse menu. Every time I mistakenly pass by the local high school around noon time, I get stuck in traffic. The high school kids leave their campus to eat. Oh my, how things have changed! The parents of some of my schoolmates were Mexican immigrants. When I would visit their homes, the parents would speak Spanish. Although I could understand what they were saying, I never thought about their prior lives in Mexico. As Mexican immigrants, they were attempting to re-establish their lives. My concern was hanging out with their sons. Thinking back, my elementary school years were on the heels of the demise of the U.S-Mexico Bracero Program (1942-1964). I attended Our Lady of Guadalupe from 1964-1971. I started Catholic high school in the fall of 1971.

---

[1] I completed my dissertation in 1999. The title of my dissertation was "A Study of Industry Location and Occupational Segmentation of Latinos and Non-Latinos in the Los Angeles Labor Market, 1980-1990."

During my childhood school days, Mexican immigrants socially and culturally replenished the community back then, and even more so now (Basok, 2000; Reichert and Massey, 1982). Indeed, Reichert and Massey (1982) explain this phenomenon regarding the ties to the Mexican American communities in the United States resulting from bracero migration:

> *First, the Bracero Program provided Mexican migrants with valuable experience in the United States' economic structure, and at the same time familiarized them with U.S. cultural and social institutions. More important, it allowed Mexican workers the opportunity to establish contacts with employers, and to build ties with Mexican American communities in the United States. In short, braceros were able to build up a network of interpersonal relations and social ties upon which future migration could and, indeed, did eventually become self-sustaining in the absence of active recruitment by the United States.*

The post-bracero era allowed two things to occur: either remain in the United States as legal residents or come back as undocumented immigrants. The bracero migration provided the opportunity to secure relationships with former employers or establish family ties. Reichert and Massey (1982) suggest the following:

> *Those who had been able to develop ties with a U.S. employer, or had established a kinship relationship with a citizen or resident alien, made use of the connections to acquire permanent resident status in the United States. Many who were unable to adjust their status in this way became illegal migrants. Indeed, the immigration statistics for the early 1960s, the time in which the Bracero Program was being phrased-out, revealed a marked increase in both the number of resident visas granted and the number of apprehensions of illegal entry.*

This chapter adds some final thoughts to immigration from Mexico. Demographic projections suggest Mexican immigration will continue the current trend of long-term migration (Jonsson and Rendall, 2004). Mexicans will be the bulk of newcomers to the United States. Mexico is a young country. Indeed, the largest age group of Mexicans is birth to five years (Castaneda, 2008). The United States is an aging country. The baby boom generation marches closer to retirement each year. The braceros interviewed for this book first came as pioneering migrants (Samora, 1971; Bustamante, 1975; Cardenas, 1975; Driscoll de Alvarado, 1999). Their legacy after the end of the program continued to be examined by immigration scholars (Bustamante, 1997; Rodriguez, 2004; Sherman, 1999; Martin, 1998). However, that does not explain their current status. As I suggested earlier (Introduction), now forty to sixty years removed from their status as guest workers, they are retired and/or living their elderly years in the United States. During previous decades they continued to migrate (Corneluis, 1978; Mines, 1979). Today, those physically able return to Mexico, but as the years pass fewer go. Previous studies documented their circular migration when these former guest workers were active within the labor market (Bean, Corona, Tuiran, Woodrow-Lafield and van Hook, 2001; Constant and Zimmerman, 2007). In short, their formative years as *active* participants in the labor market has come and gone. What we learn from their stories is the long-term effects, settlement. Documenting their stories is crucial before they are lost forever. As elderly former migrants, their stories offer insight into the migration process (Garlarza, 1964; Samora, 1971; Jenkins, 1977; Corneluis, 1992, Marcelli and Corneluis, 2001). Initially, braceros arrived as pioneering immigrants and afterwards brought their wives and the children (Dinerman, 1978; Boyd, 1989).[2] With over two million braceros contracted, there are many lives affected by the program. A *Sacramento Bee* article by reporter Susan Ferriss (2008) explains the former program's extension into the Mexican American community:

> *California is also home to most of the descendents of those who subsequently immigrated. Almost anyone in California's large Mexican American population—more than one-third of the state—can trace a family tie to a bracero.*

Just recently the Bracero Program was in the national news. A lawsuit to settle the lost 10 percent of wages from the first wave of braceros (1942-1947) had been settled (Ferris, 2008). Former braceros had until January 5, 2009 to complete the application. According to my inquiries of braceros and their family members, the required information was riddled with various arbitrary requirements. It was not uncommon to hear stories of frequent trips to the Mexican Counsel (Ferriss, 2009). Or in some cases, braceros who had gained U.S. citizenship had to renounce it. The awarding of $3,500.00 dollars to secure the lost wages was not a substantial amount given the time and interest lapsed.

I do not wish to end this book with public policy proposals already circulating (Biggs, 2004).[3] Mexican immigration is not going to exhaust itself. Mexico continues to industrialize, reaching new levels of economic development. Mexico will remain a neighbor of the United States indefinitely. How we determine public policy will reveal how humane a society we are. Reviewing our past public policies does not bode well regarding future migration. Indeed, it suggests repeating the same knee jerk reactions and proposing legislation that is counter to both sides (Massey, Durand, and Malone, 2002). Mexican migration is too complex for shorted-sighted public policies.

In summary, another U.S-Mexico Guest Worker Program would ensure some of the inherent problems already identified (Martin, 2002; Reubens, 1986; Basok, 2000). Below are some (not all of them) of the issues likely to resurface should another program become public policy:

1. Create competition or displacement of low-wage Americans by guest workers.

2. Non-enforcement of laws to ensure that employers do not hire undocumented workers outside the guest worker program.

---

[2] I am collecting the oral histories of bracero wives and their children. I will write a book on each of their experiences. Similar to their husbands, I argue that the wives of braceros were pioneering migrants before recent studies of women who entered the migration stream.

[3] For examples of guest worker proposals see Vernon M. Briggs. 2004. Guest Worker Programs: Lessons from the Past and Warnings for the Future, Center for Immigration Studies and Manuel Garcia y Griego. 2003. Mexico and U.S. Guest Workers Proposal in 2000. In California Institute for Rural Studies. Davis, California. Working Papers.

3. Not provide guarantee of livable conditions where guest workers would be housed while in the United States.

4. Opposition to pathway to citizenship. Opposed by those fearful of immigrants who are racially and culturally different from dominant *American* characteristics.

5. Long-term settlement of former guest workers with or without legal documentation.

6. Over supply of guest workers not earning enough money to ensure their efforts are worth the time and effort to contract.

7. Discrimination or hate crimes could escalate associated with nativism already targeting Mexicans in the United States.

8. Employers will threaten deportation or withholding wages if guest workers complain about their working conditions.

9. Non-guarantee working conditions are humane and not life threatening to workers.

10. Work that is outside the agreement of the contract.

11. Pay equal to current wages and adjusted for inflation.

12. Food that is eatable and served in sanitary conditions. Workers given ample time to eat their meals without having to rush or miss meals.

Today, braceros are beyond being pioneering immigrants (Jenkins, 1977). They are no longer entering into segmented labor markets, but have retired (or retiring) from them (Portes and Bach, 1985). They are not active members of the world systems model as workers or migrating immigrants (Bean, Edmonston and Passel, 1990). No longer active workers or migrating between Mexico and the United States, I argue the social capital theory model is appropriate for explaining this aging population.

Decades prior, they were actively migrating and working (Massey and Mines, 1985). Former braceros have reached their elderly years (Cohen, Forthcoming). Some continue to marginally work, but not as actively as during their formative years. They have passed the torch to the next generation of Mexican immigrants. Surviving in the current economic dire times is difficult for Mexican immigrants. The diversity of migrants includes not only males, but also female migrants, and often their children. Mexican immigration is complex and public policy that offers a band aid solution is not the answer. Below are my final thoughts on the ramifications of Mexican migration.

Current Public Discussion

As recent as President Bush's State of the Union speech in 2007, he proposed the idea of a guest worker program. Each U.S. president since the end of the former Bracero Program has considered a solution to Mexican immigration. Current U.S. Census estimates that Mexican immigrants crossing to the United States will continue well into this century. Indeed, estimates suggest that Latinos will be 125 million of the U.S. population by 2050. A large portion will be of Mexican origin. Without a secured economic plan, migration north will be the safety valve employed by Mexican surplus labor. Beyond the cost-benefits of Mexican immigration, there are the kinship ties in the United States (Barajas, 2009; Smith 2006).

As of this writing, it appears too early for President Obama to weigh in on his public policy on Mexican immigration. Early indications do suggest a comprehensive immigration reform plan (NCLR, 2009). However, immigration is an important topic. President Obama has his hands tied dealing with the current economic crisis. General Motors one of the largest private corporations in the world just declared bankruptcy (Sanger, Zeleny, and Vlasic, 2009). Unemployment is at an all time high. Foreclosures and personal bankruptcies continue to make headlines (Goodman and Healy, 2009). And it appears years away before the U.S. economy becomes stabilized once again.

Since the ending of the bracero program in 1964, undocumented immigration went unabated until the 1986 IRCA (*Immigration Reform and Control Act*) was signed by Republican President Ronald Reagan. However, immigration scholars have documented that migration was only partially slowed until it began to renew itself by the early 1990s (Orrenius and Zavodny, 2004).

Research suggests Mexican immigrants migrating to non-traditional regions such as the South and East Coast (Smith, 2006; Zuniga and Hernandez-Leon, 2006). New locations opened up as recruiters continued to fill jobs that Americans label as "immigrant jobs." Events along the border where vigilante groups are taking the law into their own hands escalate the potential for immigrant abuse. These unlawful acts intensify a crucial need to propose a viable agreement between Mexico and the United States. Acts of violence toward Mexican immigrants occur along the border on a daily basis. Besides the crimes of rape, robberies, and illegal drug deals, shootings toward lawful immigrants are not reported. Studies regarding the number of annual deaths along the border estimates that 200 to 300 undocumented immigrants perish each year (Corneluis, 2001; Eschbach, Hagan, Rodriguez, Hernandez-Leon and Bailey 1999). However, the deaths are not considered important enough to warrant a federal investigation.

More recent events, such as the massive protests against proposed legislation HR 4437, energized the Latino community. Thousands of undocumented immigrants hit the streets of major cities to protest the bill. If the bill had been passed, it would have criminalized undocumented immigrants. In addition, the bill would have punished those who assisted undocumented immigrants. Estimates suggest that 11 to 12 million undocumented immigrants currently live and work in the United States (Preston, 2009). The majority of the undocumented immigrants are from Mexico.

Ever since the dismantling of the former Bracero Program in 1964, there have been numerous proposals for a renewed guest worker program (Hedges, 2003). One of the barriers to a guest worker program has been the amnesty portion. Those who oppose amnesty argue that it gives an unfair and unearned advantage to law breakers. Those who support the amnesty portion argue that it allows for immigrants to legalize their status after years of working and showing themselves contributing to their communities. Only a sound rational public policy debate is warranted. Until then, Mexican immigration will continue to make headlines and nothing will be solved in the long run.

A Special Case—Don Refugio "Cuco" Gonzalez

This book examining the former Bracero Program was both a personal and historical documentation. Indeed, the final story is related to how the book became bigger than I had imagined. The story involves my father's friendship with Don Refugio "Cuco" Gonzalez. To begin, I do not want to suggest that Don "Cuco's" story is representative of all braceros who participated in the program. But it helps to illustrate how, over time, migration can become the initial step toward settlement. Migrating through the Bracero Program for more than a decade, Don "Cuco" and my father became friends. Don "Cuco" was my first bracero interview. I want to thank him for being willing to recount his story. I have to admit I was apprehensive regarding interviewing him. I was testing my idea of oral histories being the correct method to examine the legacy of braceros. It was a family occasion as my parents joined us on that historic day. I did interview him again to qualify some answers and to make sure it was done under the right conditions.

During my childhood, I recall how, out of the blue, Don "Cuco" would appear at my parents' house. Only a brief phone call before he would come over would warn us of pending company. As children, not really sure who this family was, we were always expected to greet them and sit quietly as the grownups spoke. It was the only time we would be able to sit in the living room. Even today when I take a drink or snack into my parents' living room, I can feel my mother's presence come along. The room was off limits to us. To be able to sit in the living room with the adults meant it was a special occasion.

Don "Cuco" was among the few chosen because there were so many others who were turned away. Below he retells his contracting experience and how he came to the border:

> The security stopped me and asked me where I was going. He told me that the office was closed and that I should come back tomorrow. I told him that I was going to the human resources office because I needed to take care of some paper work that I needed by the next day. Luckily, he allowed me to go into the office before they closed. I got there just in time. The assistant looked at all my paperwork but told me to come back again the next day. . . . I came back the next day and pulled out the pass that the lady had previously given me. I went to the front of the line and the American Consulate assisted me. They asked me why I wanted to come to the U.S. I told them that I wanted to come in order to work.
>
> What's your work status as of now?
>
> I again told them that I did different jobs for different people and also worked in the fields.
>
> And your family, are you thinking of taking them along?
>
> Not at this moment, I told them . . .
>
> The Embassy gave me a certificate that I needed to carry with me at all times. I returned home and ran into my brother. I told him everything that had happened and he was happy for me. . . . The day soon arrived when I had to come to the U.S. On the way, I met a man from a local town that had head-

ed in the same direction and we decided to come along... In Guadalajara we boarded a bus on its way to Mexicali. We stopped in a town called Santana to board another bus. It was around 5 or 6 p.m. We waited and waited for the next bus around 1 a.m. It was chaos. The driver did not look presentable at all. His hair was uncombed, his clothes were dirty, and his eyes were red. It may have been for lack of sleep or who knows. No one trusted the driver but we still came along praying to God for a safe trip.... The road was not the best road. It was an unpaved road and you can imagine the ride. We hardly got any sleep. I was sitting on the driver's side in case anything happened. Soon enough the unexpected happened. The bus somehow got off the road and flipped. Luckily enough, the door was used as an emergency escape. I broke the glass and opened the door. We all tried to run out bringing important belongings. I always carried my certificate in my pocket and ran out without bringing my backpack. .. It was a moment of panic because we all thought that the bus was going to explode. We all came out safe except for the bus driver. Soon enough, he came out and tried to run away. Forced to return, he came back. We waited for aid from six in the morning to about ten. From there, we were sent to a station in Sonora where shamelessly an assistant asked us how many dead people we had brought with us. . . . We all complained because we knew that the bus driver had been drunk and we could prove it because of the smell. You were able to smell the liquor. The supervisor soon came out to assist us and we gave him the whole rundown of what had happened from Guadalajara to the crash site. He explained to us that the bus we had come in was not made to climb hills and mountains. That was the reason it had flipped over. He gave us a lot of nonsense. . . .

This is the story of how I received all my documents. I only ended up paying $800 pesos. The letter of recommendation from Charlie had been a great help. A lot of the rancheros gave the letters for free while others sold them. However it was, it was something that I really deserved. I believe that is the reason why I matured so fast. I tell people so that they may know what the Bracero Program was about and how I got to experience it. I experienced the real stuff. From the beginning, I knew how to survive. I worked fourteen years without ever having a problem.

Through personal contacts or social networks, braceros were able to continue to migrate. Don "Cuco" was contracted to work at the ranch where my father worked and where my family lived for ten years. He worked there until the program ended. He eventually returned to Mexico to be with his family. The story of Don "Cuco" and his family reflects that a temporary guest worker program is inherently a permanent proposition.

My father's relationship with Don "Cuco" provided advice on what to do regarding his family back in Mexico. At the time, when he would come to visit, I did not know he was attempting to decide whether to relocate his family in the United States. But the frequent visits by his family to our house suggested he was considering it. During one of my visits to acquire Don "Cuco's" oral history, he revealed how he had met other braceros and remained in contact with them:

Don Cuco: You should get in touch with Chuy Hernandez and his wife. I'm sure they also have good stories

Paul: Well, you met their family right?

Don Cuco: Yes, we met at church and then met their whole family. We also came in the same train.

Paul: Did his brother come? Roberto Santillano?

Don Cuco: I think he did. He may live in Santa Barbara. I know a few braceros that have married into families. Pancho married a daughter of the Ibarras; they are related to the Borrayos.

Paul: Yes I knew some Borrayos that lived in Goleta. I also know their sister Rasario y Lucia. Rosario lives in Los Angeles.

Don Cuco: Joaquin Ibarra was also a bracero. The Borrayos should know Pancho's whereabouts, Francisco Santiallan, and he may know where the brother is. Hopefully by next time you come I can have Pancho's address. Another one that can give you a good story is El Coronel, a good friend of his, who also came during the Bracero Program. He lives near Scolarie's.

Continuing my discussion with Don "Cuco," I wanted to see what role my father had in getting him to settle in the United States. Indeed, with advice from my father, he decided to settle. After years of going back and forth, he and his family made the decision to settle permanently.

Paul: Why did you decide to come and make the U.S. your home?

Don Cuco: I decided to come to the U.S. because I kept asking your dad how his family was doing and what type of education they were getting. I liked all that he was telling me and since I had a big family I decided to come and bring them. What I had in Mexico was just not sufficient to survive. I wanted to try the new life and God really helped me. Now I'm living the best life I can imagine including my family.

Finally, I asked Don "Cuco" how he felt about his permanent status in the United States. According to immigration scholars, over time, former immigrants will establish long-term ties to the host country. There is no better indicator of long-term settlement than when children of immigrants establish lives as native-born citizens. In short, I wanted to know how he saw his kids who now are settled in the United States.

Paul: What do your kids call themselves, Mexicans or Americans?

Don Cuco: Well, I have two that are American citizens, the rest were residents but now they have become citizens. This is something we have to thank Pete Wilson for. He was the one that brought about green card renewals with a $70 fee for every ten years. Instead of doing this every ten years, we all decided to become citizens. This is what motivated me to become a citizen. I preferred to become a citizen instead of wasting $70 every ten years. I also get more benefits as a citizen when it comes to my pensions.

Conclusion

This chapter attempted to put the immigration debate into perspective. Regardless of your opinion on immigration from Mexico, the short- or long-term analysis suggests that migration will continue. The bigger question is: Can we find a reasonable means to control the flow? Regulating the number of Mexican immigrants crossing is a daunting task. But to secure the border, it must be done. One solution consists of making the demand of migration less of an option. For Mexico, that means extensive economic investment by the United States and other foreign countries. But investments that provide stable jobs and livable wages. Of course that is easier said than done. The economic concern of investment corporations operating in Mexico is to make a profit.

The bracero oral histories offered insight into migration and settlement. The age of braceros today makes it imperative that their stories be told. Of course this is only one side of the story. The other side of the story, I suppose, would come from braceros who decided not to stay permanently in the United States. Rather they chose to return to Mexico to live out their elderly years.

Should another guest worker program between the United States and Mexico occur, it would be my view that many of the inherent problems heard in the stories revealed in this book would be renewed. Although there continues to be an anti-immigrant sentiment toward Mexicans, there are Mexican immigrants crossing, as of this writing. The trend continues and follows more than two centuries of migration (Garcia 1981; Barajas, 2009).

Finally, this book also examined how families, such as my own and others, were affected by the program. Each of the families that I contacted for the oral interviews included in this book had similar stories; indeed, stories of contracting through the former program and leaving Mexico for permanent settlement in the United States. I have little doubt that the stories my father and mother told me are similar to other Chicano and Mexican families. The time and circumstances were likely different, but the same pattern of settlement was likely the same. In short, this book is another view of how the American story continues to play out. Mexican immigrants and their descendants are fulfilling the destiny of other immigrants before and after them. In the case of Mexican immigrants, it's a story that has been ongoing since, and before, 1848.

References

Acuna, Rodolfo. 2007. *Occupied America: A History of Chicanos*. Prentice Hall.

Aguilera, Michael B. 2002. "The Impact of Social Capital on Labor Force Participation: Evidence from the 2000 Social Capital Benchmark Survey." *Social Science Quarterly* 83, pp. 853-74.

Aguilera, Michael B., and Douglas S. Massey. 2003. "Social Capital and the Wages of Mexican Migrants: New Hypotheses and Tests." *Social Forces*, Vol. 82, No. 2, pp. 671-701.

Almaguer, Tomas. 2008. *Racial Fault Lines: The Historical Origins of White Supremacy in California*. University of California Press.

Archibold, Randal C. 2006. "Immigrants Take to U.S. Streets in Show of Strength." *New York Times*.

Balderama, Francisco and Raymond Rodriguez. 1996. *Decade of Betrayal: Mexican Repatriation in the 1930s*. University of New Mexico Press.

Barajas, Manuel.2009. *The Xaripu Community across Borders: Labor Migration, Community and Family*. Notre Dame. University of Notre Dame Press.

Barrera, Mario. 1979. *Race and Class in the Southwest: A Theory of Racial Inequality*. University of Notre Dame Press.

Basok, Tanya. 2000. "He Came, He Saw, He ... Stayed. Guest Worker Programmes and the Issue of Non-Return." *International Migration*. Vol. 38, Issue 2, pp. 215-238.

Bautista-Hayes, David. 2004. *La Nueva California: Latinos in the Golden State*. Berkeley, CA. University of California Press.

Bean, Frank D., Rodolfo Corona, Rodolfo Tuiran, Karen A. Woodrow-Lafield, Jennifer van Hook. 2001. "Circular, Invisible, and Ambiguous Migrants: Components of Difference in Estimates of the Number of Unauthorized Mexican Migrants in the United States." *Demography*, Vol. 38, No. 3, pp. 411-422.

Bean Frank D; Edmonston Barry; and Passel Jeffery, S. 1990. *Undocumented Migration to the United States: IRCA and the Experience of the 1980s*. Rand Corporation.

Bloomekatz, Ari B. 2008. "Ex-Braceros get 2 months to File Claims for up to $3,500: A Class Action Settlement for Mexicans who worked in the U.S. during WWII may affect 20,000 still living in this Country." *Los Angeles Times*.

Bonacich, Edna. 1973. "A Theory of Middleman Minorities." *American Sociological Review*, Vol. 38, No. 5, pp. 583-594.

Boyd, Monica. 1989. "Family and Personal Networks in International Migration: Recent Developments and New Agendas." *International Migration Review*, Vol. 23, No. 3, Special Silver Anniversary Issue: *International Migration an Assessment for the 90's*, pp. 638-670

Bourdieu, Pierre. 1986. "The Forms of Capital." In *Handbook of Theory and Research for the Sociology of Education*, edited by John G. Richardson. Greenwood Press.

Briggs, Vernon, Jr. 2004. "Guestworker Programs: Lessons From the Past and Warnings for the Future." *Backgrounder*. Center for Immigration Studies.

Buchanan, Patrick. 2002. *The Death of the West: How Dying Populations and Immigrant Invasions Imperil Our Country and Civilization*. St. Martin's Griffin.

Bustamante, Jorge A. 1977. "Undocumented Immigration from Mexico: Research Report." *International Migration Review,* Vol. 11, No. 2, pp. 149-177.

Bustamante, Jorge A. 1975. "Espaldas Mojados; Materia Prima para la Expansion del Capital Norteamericaiso." *Cuadernos del CES*, Series, No. 9. Mexico: El Colegio de Mexico.

Calavita, Kitty. 1992. *Inside the State: The Bracero Program, Immigration and the INS*. Routledge, Chapman and Hall.

Cardenas, Gilberto. 1975. "United States Immigration Policy Toward Mexico: An Historical Perspective." *Chicano/Latino Law Review* 2, pp. 66-91.

Cardoso, Lawrence. 1980. *Mexican Emigration to the United States, 1897-1931: Socio-Economic Patterns.* University of Arizona Press.

Castaneda, Jorge G. 2008. *Ex Mex: From Migrants to Immigrants*. New Press.

Castles, Stephen. 1986. "The Guest-Worker in Western Europe—An Obituary." *International Migration Review*, Vol. 20, No. 4, Special Issue: *Temporary Worker Programs: Mechanisms, Conditions, Consequences*, pp. 761-778.

Cerrutti, Marcela and Douglas S. Massey. 2004. "Trends in Mexican Migration to the United States, 1965-1995." In Jorge Durand and Douglas S. Massey, (eds.), *Crossing the Border: Research from the Mexican Migration Project*. New York: Russell Sage.

Chavez, Leo, R. 2008. *The Latino Threat: Constructing Immigrants, Citizens, and the Nation*. Stanford University Press.

Chavez, Leo, R. 1993. *Shadowed Lives: Undocumented Immigrants in American Society*. Fort Worth, Texas: Harcourt, Brace and Jovanovich College Publishers.

Chiswick, Barry R. 1999. "Are Immigrants Favorably Self-Selected?" *The American Economic Review*, Vol. 89, No. 2, pp. 181-185.

Chiswick, Barry. 1991. "Speaking, Reading, and Earnings among Low-Skilled Immigrants" *Journal of Labor Economics*, Vol. 9, No. 2, pp. 149-170.

Cohen, Deborah. Forthcoming. "Outside the Border of the Modern: Mexican Migration and the Racialized and Gendered Dynamics of US' National Belonging." Chapter from *Transnational Subjects*. University of North Carolina University Press.

Cohen, Deborah. 2006. "From Peasant to Worker: Migration, Masculinity, and the Making of Mexican Workers in the US." *International Labor and Working-Class History* No. 69, 2006, pp. 81–103.

Coleman, James S. 1988. "Social Capital in the Creation of Human Capital." *American Journal of Sociology*.

Constant, Amelie and Klaus F. Zimmermann. 2007. *Circular Migration: Counts of Exits and Years Away from the Host Country*. Institute for the Study of Labor. pp. 1-23.

Corneluis, Wayne. 1992. *From Sojourners to Settlers: The Changing Profile of Mexican Immigration to the United States*. Center for US-Mexican Studies, University of California.

Corneluis, Wayne. 1993. "Mexicans in California Today." In Ivan Light and Parminder (eds.), *Immigration and Entrepreneurship: Culture, Capital, and Ethnic Networks*. Transaction Publishers.

Corneluis, Wayne. 1981. "Mexican Migration to the United States." *Proceedings of the Academy of Political Science*, Vol. 34, No. 1, Mexico-United States Relations, pp. 67-77.

Corneluis, Wayne. 2001. "Death at the Border: Efficacy and Unintended Consequences of US Immigration Control Policy." *Population and Development Review*, Vol. 27, No. 4, pp. 666-685.

Cornelius, Wayne A. 1989. "Impacts of the 1986 US Immigration Law on Emigration from Rural Mexican Sending Communities." *Population and Development Review*, Vol. 15, No. 4, pp. 689-705.

Craig, Richard. 1971. *The Bracero Program*. Austin: University of Texas Press.

Daniels, Roger. 2002. *Coming to America: A History of Immigration and Ethnicity in American Life.* Harper Perennial; 2nd edition.

De Leon, Arnold. 1983. *They Called Greasers: Anglo Attitudes Toward Mexicans in Texas, 1821-1900.* University of Texas Press.

Dinerman, Ian R. 1978. "Patterns of Adaptation among Households of U.S.-Bound Migrants from Michoacan, Mexico." *International Migration Review*, Vol. 12, No. 4, Special Issue: *Illegal Mexican Immigrants to the United States*, pp. 485-501.

Donato, Katharine M., Brandon Wagner, and Evelyn Patterson. 2008. "The Cat and Mouse Game at the Mexico-U.S. Border: Gendered Patterns and Recent Shifts." *International Migration Review*, Volume 42, Issue 2, pp. 330-359.

Donato, Katharine M. and E. Patterson 2006. "A Glass Half Full? Gender in Migration Studies." *International Migration Review*. 40, pp. 3–26.

Driscoll, Barbara. 1999. *The Tracks North: The Railroad Bracero Program of World War II*. University of Texas Press.

Durand, Jorge and Douglas S. Massey. 1992. "Mexican Migration to the United States: A Critical Review." *Latin American Research Review*. Vol. 27, No. 2 (1992), pp. 3-42.

Durand, Jorge, Douglas S. Massey, and Fernando Charvet. 2000. "The Changing Geography of Mexican Immigration to the United States: 1910-1996." *Social Science Quarterly* 81, pp. 1-15.

Durand, Jorge, Douglas S. Massey, and Emilio A. Parrado. 1999. "The New Era of Mexican Migration to the United States." *The Journal of American History*. Vol. 86, No. 2. A Special Issue, pp. 518-536.

Eschbach, Karl, Jacqueline Hagan, Nestor Rodriguez, Rafael Hernandez-Leon and Stanley Bailey. 1999. "Death at the Border." *International Migration Review*, Vol. 33, No. 2, pp. 430-454.

Ewing, Walter. 1999. "A New Bracero Program for the 21st Century." *The Washington Report on the Hemisphere 19* (19): Washington: D.C.

Ferraez, Jorge. 2003. "David Hayes-Bautista: the end of California as we know it"—*Q&A Latino Leaders: The National Magazine of the Successful American Latino.*

Ferriss, Susan. 2009. "Deadline Monday to Claim Reimbursement for Former Braceros." *Sacramento Bee.*

Ferriss, Susan. 2008. "Braceros line up for wages withheld during WWII." *Sacramento Bee.*

Flores, Estevan T. 1984. "Research on Undocumented Immigrants and Public Policy: A Study of the Texas School Case." *International Migration Review*, Vol. 18, No. 3, Special Issue: *Irregular Migration: An International Perspective* (Autumn, 1984), pp. 505-523.

Furillo, Andy. 2001. "The Longer Farm Workers Stay, the Sicker They Get: Legal Immigrants Suffer from Greater Chronic Health Problems, A New UC Study Reveals." *Sacramento Bee.*

Gamboa, Erasmo. 2000. *Mexican Labor & World War II: Braceros in the Pacific Northwest, 1942-1947.* University of Washington Press.

Gamboa, Erasmo. 1987. "Braceros in the Pacific Northwest: Laborers on the Domestic Front, 1942-1947." *Pacific Historical Review* 61, pp. 378-398.

Gamio, Manuel. 1930. *The Mexican Immigrant, His Life-Story; Autobiographic Documents.* Chicago, Ill., The University of Chicago Press.

Garcia Y Griego, Manuel. 1996. "The Importation of Mexican Contract Laborers to the United States, 1942-1964: Antecedents, Operations and Legacy." In David G. Gutiérrez (ed)., *Between Two Worlds: Mexican Immigrants in the United States.* Wilmington, Delaware, Scholarly Resources.

García, Juan Ramon. 1981. *Operation Wetback: The Mass Deportation of Mexican Undocumented Workers in 1954.* University of California Press

Garcia, Mario, T. 1989. *Mexican Americans: Leadership, Ideology, and Identity, 1930-1960.* Yale University Press.

Garcia, Mario, T. 1982. *Desert Immigrants; The Mexicans of El Paso, 1880-1920.* Yale University Press.

Garcia, Jerry and Gilbert Garcia. 2005. "The Racialization of Mexican and Japanese Labor in the Pacific Northwest." In *Memory, Community, and Activism: Mexican Migration and Labor in the Pacific Northwest.* Julian Samora Research Institute and Michigan State University.

Garlarza, Ernesto. 1977. *The Tragedy at Chualar.* Santa Barbara, CA: McNally and Loftin.

Garlarza, Ernesto. 1964. *Merchants of Labor: The Mexican Bracero Story.* Santa Barbara, CA. McNally and Loftin.

Green, Susan Marie. 1997. *Zoot Suiters: Past and Present.* University of Minnesota, 1997, Ph.D. Thesis.

Gonzalez, Manuel, G. 2009. *Mexicanos: A History of Mexicans in the United States.* University of Indiana Press.

Gonzalez, Gilberto G., and Raul Fernandez. 2003. *A Century of Chicano History: Empire, Nations and Migration.* Routledge Press.

Gomez-Quinones, Juan. 1994. *Mexican American Labor, 1790-1990.* Albuquerque. University of New Mexico Press.

Gonzalez Gilberto. 2007. *Guest Workers or Colonized Labor?: Mexican Labor Migration to the United States.* Paradigm Publishers.

Goodman, Peter S., and Jack Healy. 2009. "Job Losses Push Safer Mortgages to Foreclosure." *New York Times.*

Grassmuck Sherri, and Patricia R. Pessar. *Between Two Islands: Dominican International Migration.* University of California Press.

Grey, Mark A. and Anne C. Woodrick. 2002. "Unofficial sister cities: Meatpacking labor migration between Villachuato, Mexico, and Marshalltown, IA." *Human Organization*, 61, pp. 364-376.

Hahamovitch, Cindy. 1999. "The Politics of Labor Scarcity: Expediency and the Birth of the Agricultural 'Guestworkers' Program." Center for Immigration Studies. *Backgrounders.*

Hanson, Victor Davis. 2003. *Mexifornia: A State of Becoming. A State of Becoming.* Encounter Books.

Hedges, Michael. 2003. "Cornyn set to outline Guest Worker Program." *Houston Chronicle* Washington Bureau.

Hondagneu-Sotelo, Pierrette. 2007. *Domesticas; Immigrant Workers Cleaning and Caring in the Shadows of Affluence.* Berkeley: University of California Press.

Hondagneu-Sotelo, Pierrette. 1994. *Gender Transitions. Mexican Experiences of Immigration.* Berkeley: University of California Press.

Hondagneu-Sotelo, Pierrette. 1997. "The History of Mexican Undocumented Settlement in the United States." In *Challenging Fronteras: Structuring Latina and Latino Lives in the U.S.* Edited by Mary Romero, Pierrette Hondagneu-Sotelo and Vilma Ortiz. New York: Routledge.

Hopfensperger, Jean. 2009. "Hard Times Send Latinos Back Across the Border Fewer Jobs, Tougher Immigration Rules Force Some Immigrants to Return Home." *Star Tribune*.

Jenkins, J. Craig. 1977. "Push/Pull in Recent Mexican Migration to the U.S." *International Migration Review*, Vol. 11, No. 2, pp. 178-189.

Jonsson, Stefan Hrafn and Michael S. Rendall. 2004. The Fertility Contribution of Mexican Immigration to the United States. *Demography*. Vol. 41, No. 1, pp. 129-150.

Kirstein, Peter N. 1979. *Anglo over Bracero: A History of the Mexican Worker in the United States from Roosevelt to Nixon*. San Francisco, CA. R and E Research Associates.

Kiser, George and David Silverman, 1973. "Mexican Repatriation During the Great Depression." *Journal of Mexican American History*, pp. 139-164.

Klein, Naomi. 2008. *Shock Doctrine: The Rise of Disaster Capitalism*. Vintage Canada.

Kossoudji, Sherrie A. 1992. "Playing Cat and Mouse at the U.S.-Mexican Border." *Demography*, Vol. 29, No. 2, pp. 159-180.

Light, Ivan. 2004. "Immigration and Ethnic Economies in Giant Cities." *International Social Science Journal* 181, pp. 385-398.

Light, Ivan. 1972. *Ethnic Enterprise in America*. Berkeley and Los Angeles: University of California.

Levitt, Peggy. 2001 *The Transnational Villagers*. Berkeley and Los Angeles: University of California Press.

Levitt, Peggy and Mary Waters. 2002 *The Changing Face of Home: The Transnational Lives of the Second Generation*. New York: Russell Sage Foundation.

Malkin, Elisabeth. 2007. "Graft Mars the Recruitment of Mexican Guest Workers." *New York Times*.

Marcelli, Enrico A. and Wayne A. Cornelius. 2001. "The Changing Profile of Mexican Migrants to the United States: New Evidence from California and Mexico." *Latin American Research Review*, Vol. 36, No. 3, pp. 105-131.

Martin, Philip. 2001. "The Mirage of Mexican Guest Workers." *Foreign Affairs* 80, pp. 1.

Martin, Philip. 1998. "Guest Workers: Past and Present." In *Mexico-United States Binational Migration Study, Migration Between Mexico and the United States*, Volume 3, Washington, D.C.: U.S. Commission on Immigration Reform and Mexican Ministry of Foreign Affairs, pp. 877-896.

Martin, Philip. 2002. "Mexican Workers and U.S. Agriculture: The Revolving Door." *International Migration Review*, Vol. 36, No. 4, Host Societies and the Reception of Immigrants: Institutions, Markets and Policies, pp. 1124-1142.

Martin, Philip L., and Michael S. Teitelbaum. 2001. "The Mirage of Mexican Guest Workers." *Foreign Affairs*. November/December 2001.

Massey, Douglas. 1987. "Understanding Mexican Migration to the United States." *Journal of American Sociology* 92, pp. 1372-1403.

Massey, Douglas and Jorge Durand. 2004. *Crossing the Border: Research from the Mexican Migration Project*. New York: Russell Sage Foundation.

Massey, Douglas, Rafael Alacorn, Jorge Durand, Humberto Gonzalez. 1987. *Return to Aztlan: The Social Process of International Migration from Western Mexico*. Berkeley and Los Angeles: University of California Press.

Massey, Douglas, S., and Richard Mines. 1985. "A Comparison of Patterns of U.S. Migration in Two Mexican Sending Communities." *Latin American Research Review* 20, p. 123.

Massey, Douglas, S., and Zai Liang. 1989. "The Long-Term Consequences of a Temporary Worker Program: The U.S. Bracero Program." *Population Research and Public Policy* 8, pp. 199-226.

Massey, Douglas. 2007. "Immigration: Policy of Contradiction." *Sacramento Bee.*

Massey, Douglas S. 1987. "Understanding Mexican Migration to the United States." *Journal of American Sociology* 92, p. 1403.

Massey, Douglas S, and Jorge Durand. (eds). 2004 *Crossing the Border: Research from the Mexican Migration Project.* New York: Russell Sage Foundation.

Massey, Douglas S, Jorge Durand, and Fernando Charvet. 2000. "The Changing Geography of Mexican Immigration to the United States: 1910-1996" *Social Science Quarterly* 81.

Massey, Douglas S, Jorge Durand and Nolan Malone. 2002 *Beyond Smoke and Mirrors: Mexican Immigration in an Age of Economic Integration.* New York: Russell Sage Foundation.

McWilliams, Carey. 1975. *North From Mexico.* Praeger Publishers.

Mines, Richard and Douglas Dassey. 1985. "Patterns of Migration to the United States from Two Mexican Communities." *Latin American Research Review*, Vol. 20, No. 2, pp. 104-123.

Mize, Ronald L. (2006). "Mexican Contract Workers and the U.S. Capitalist Agricultural Labor Process: The Formative Era, 1942-1964." *Rural Sociology.* 71, pp. 85-107.

NCLR. 2009. "National Council of La Raza Joins National Immigration Campaign to Push for Immigration Solutions." News Release.

Nevins, Joseph. 2002. *Operation Gatekeeper: The Rise of the "illegal Alien" and the Making of the U.S.- Mexico Boundary.* Routledge.

Orrenius, Pia M. and Madeline Zavodny. 2005. "Self-Selection among Undocumented Immigrants from Mexico." *Journal of Development Economics,* October 78, pp. 215-240.

Passel, Jeffrey S. and Karen A. Woodrow. 1987. "Change in the Undocumented Alien Population in the United States, 1979-1983." *International Migration Review*, Vol. 21, No. 4, Special Issue: *Measuring International Migration: Theory and Practice.* pp. 1304-1334.

Peach, James and Williams James. 2000. "Population and economics dynamics on the U.S.-Mexican border: Past, present and future." In: Ganster P. (ed.), *The U.S.-Mexican Border Environment: A Road Map to a Sustainable 2020.*

Piore, Michael. 1979. *Birds of Passage: Migrant Labor and Industrial Societies.* Cambridge, England, Cambridge Univ. Press.

Pitt, Leonard. 1966. *The Decline of the Californios; a social history of the Spanish-speaking Californians, 1846-1890.* Berkeley, University of California Press.

Porter, Eduardo and Elisabeth Malkin. 2005. "Mexicans at Home Abroad." *New York Times.*

Portes, Alejandro. 1994. "Introduction: Immigration and Its Aftermath." *International Migration Review*, Vol. 28, No. 4, Special Issue: *The New Second Generation,* pp. 632-639.

Portes, Alejandro. 1994. "The Informal Economy and Its Paradoxes." In Neil J. Smelser and Richard. Swedberg (eds.), *Handbook of Economic Sociology.* pp. 426-449. Princeton, NJ: Princeton University Press.

Portes, Alejandro and Robert Bach. 1985. *Latin Journey.* University of California Press.

Portes, Alejandro, Luis E. Guarnizo, and Patricia Landolt. 1999. "The Study of Transnationalism: Pitfalls and Promise of an Emergent Research Field." *Ethnic and Racial Studies* No. 4, pp. 217-237.

Portes, Alejandro and Ruben G. Rumbaut. 2006. *Immigrants of America: A Portrait.* Berkeley: University of California Press.

Potok, Mark. 2008. "Hope Amidst the Hate? Intelligence Report." *Southern Poverty Report.*

Preston, Julie. 2009. "Mexican Data Show Migration to U.S. in Decline." *New York Times.*

Preston, Julie. 2006. "G.O.P. in Senate Narrows Immigration Focus to 700-Mile Fence." *New York Times.*

Preston, Julie. 2006. "Pennsylvania Town Delays Enforcing Tough Immigration Law." *New York Times.*

Pulido, Alberto L., Barbara Driscoll de Alvarado, and Carmen Samora, (eds.). Forthcoming. *Moving Beyond Borders: Julian Samora and the Establishment of Latino Studies.* University of Illinois Press.

Reichert, Joshua and Douglas Massey. 1980. "History and Trends in U.S.-Bound Migration from a Mexican Town." *International Migration Review* 14, pp. 475-491.

Reichert, Joshua and Douglas Massey. 1982. "Guestworker programs: Evidence from Europe and the United States and some implications for U.S. policy." *Population Research and Policy Review.*

Reubens, Edwin P. 1986. "Temporary Foreign Workers in the U.S.: Myths, Facts and Policies." *International Migration Review,* Vol. 20, No. 4, "Special Issue: *Temporary Worker Programs: Mechanisms, Conditions, Consequences,*" pp. 1037-1047.

Roberts, Sam. 2007. "In U.S. Name Count, Garcias Are Catching Up With Joneses." *New York Times.*

Rochin, Refugio I, and Dennis Valdez. 2000. *Voices of a New Chicana/o History.* Michigan State University Press.

Rodriguez, Nestor. 2004. *"Workers Wanted" Employer Recruitment of Immigrant Labor, Work and Occupations.* Vol. 31, No. 4, pp. 453-473.

Rosas, Ana Elizabeth. *"Women and the Bracero Program," Latinas in the United States: A Historical Encyclopedia.* Edited by Vicki L. Ruiz and Virginia Sanchez-Korrol. Indiana University Press. 2006.

Ruiz, Vicki. 2008. *From Out of the Shadows: Mexican Women in Twentieth-Century America.* Oxford University Press.

Samora, Julian. 1971. *Los Mojados: The Wetback Story.* Notre Dame: The University of Notre Dame Press.

Samora, Julian. 1975. "Mexican Immigration," In Gus Tyler (ed.), *Mexican-Americans Tomorrow.* University of New Mexico Press.

Sanchez, George. 1995. *Becoming Mexican American: Ethnicity, Culture and Identity in Chicano Los Angeles, 1900-1945.* Oxford University Press.

Sanger, David E., Jeff Zeleny, and Bill Vlasic. "2009 G.M. to Seek Bankruptcy and a New Start." *New York Times.*

Sassen, Saskia. 2006. *Cities in a World Economy.* Pine Forge Press; 3rd edition.

Schmitter Heisler, Barbara. 2007. "The 'Other Braceros' Temporary Labor and GermanPrisoners of War in the United States, 1943-1946." *Social Science History.* 31, pp. 239-271.

Schlesinger, Arthur M. Jr. 1998. *The Disuniting of America: Reflections on a Multicultural Society.* W.W. Norton & Co.

Sherman, Rachel 1999. "From State Introversion to State Extension in Mexico: Modes of Emigrant Incorporation, 1900-1997." *Theory and Society.* Volume 28, Number 6, pp. 835-878.

Smith, Robert Courtney. 2006. *Mexican New York: Transnational Lives of New Immigrants.* University of California Press.

Takaki, Ronald. 2001. *Double Victory A Multicultural History of America in World War II.* Back Bay Books.

Takaki, Ronald. 1989. *A History of Asian Americans: Strangers from A Different Shore.* Back Bay Publishers.

Telles, Edward E. and Vilma Ortiz. 2008. *Generations of Exclusion: Mexican Americans, Assimilation, and Race.* Russell Sage Publications.

Tiano, Susan. 1994. *Patriarchy on the Line: Gender, Labor, and Ideology in the Mexican Maquila Industry,* Temple University Press, 1994.

Tuchman, Barbara W. *The Zimmermann Telegram.* New York: The Viking Press, 1958.

Valdez, Dennis. 2000. *Barrios Norteños: St. Paul and Midwestern Mexican Communities in the Twentieth Century.* University of Texas Press.

Valenzuela, Abel Jr. 2001. "Day Laborers as Entrepreneurs?" *Journal of Ethnic and Migration Studies, 1469-9451,* Volume 27, Issue 2, pp. 335-352.

Vargas, Zaragosa. 1999. *Proletarians of the North: Mexican Industrial Workers in Detroit and the Midwest, 1917-1933.* Berkeley: University of California Press.

Warren, Robert and Jeffery S. Passel. 1987. "A Count of the Uncountable: Estimates of Undocumented Aliens Counted in the 1980 United States Census." *Demography,* Vol. 24, No. 3, pp. 375-393.

White, Michael J., Frank D. Bean, and Thomas J. Espenshade. 1990. "The U.S. 1986 Immigration Reform and Control Act and Undocumented Immigration to the United States." *Population Research and Policy Review* 9, pp. 93-116.

Woodrow, Karen A. and Jeffery S. Passel. 1990. "Post-IRCA Undocumented Immigration to the United States: An Assessment Based on the June 1988 CPS." pp. 33-75. In *Undocumented Migration to the United States: IRCA and the Experience of the 1980s,* edited by Frank D. Bean, Barry Edmonston, and Jeffery S. Passel. Washington, DC: Urban Institute Press.

Zaragosa, Vargas. 1999. *Proletarians of the North: Mexican Industrial Workers in Detroit and the Midwest, 1917-1933.* Berkeley: University of California Press.

Zúñiga, Víctor and Rubén Hernández-León. (eds.). 2006. *New Destinations: Mexican Immigration in the United States.* Russell Sage Publications.

Zinn, Howard. 2003. *A People's History of the United States: 1492 to Present.* Harper Perennial.